MATERNITY AND PARENTAL RIGHTS
A PRACTICAL GUIDE

Katie Wood

London: The Stationery Office

Applications for reproduction should be made in writing to The Stationery Office Limited, St Crispins, Duke Street, Norwich NR3 1PD.

The information contained in this publication is believed to be correct at the time of manufacture. Whilst care has been taken to ensure that the information is accurate, the publishers can accept no responsibility for any errors or omissions or for changes to the details given.

A CIP catalogue for this book is available from the British Library.
A Library of Congress CIP catalogue record has been applied for.

First published 2001.

ISBN 0 11 702552 6

Printed in the United Kingdom by The Stationery Office
TJ3387   C10   02/01   19585   581505

Published by The Stationery Office and available from:

The Stationery Office
(mail, telephone and fax orders only)
PO Box 29, Norwich NR3 1GN
General enquiries/Telephone orders 0870 600 5522
Fax orders 0870 600 5533
www.thestationeryoffice.com

The Stationery Office Bookshops
123 Kingsway, London WC2B 6PQ
020 7242 6393 Fax 020 7242 6394
68–69 Bull Street, Birmingham B4 6AD
0121 236 9696 Fax 0121 236 9699
33 Wine Street, Bristol BS1 2BQ
0117 926 4306 Fax 0117 929 4515
9–21 Princess Street, Manchester M60 8AS
0161 834 7201 Fax 0161 833 0634
16 Arthur Street, Belfast BT1 4GD
028 9023 8451 Fax 028 9023 5401
The Stationery Office Oriel Bookshop
18–19, High Street, Cardiff CF1 2BZ
029 2039 5548 Fax 029 2038 4347
71 Lothian Road, Edinburgh EH3 9AZ
0870 606 5566 Fax 0870 606 5588

The Stationery Office's Accredited Agents
(see Yellow Pages)
and through good booksellers

CONTENTS

PREFACE

The aim of this guide is to provide employers with as clear and concise an account of the law as possible, along with examples of good maternity and parental policies. The guide sets out the minimum legal rights of employees and provides good practice options. This area of the law is notoriously complicated. Simplification and clarification would be in the interests of employers and employees alike. Areas where the law is not clear are explained as employers need to make a policy decision about the terms and conditions they wish to offer. What terms an employer offers will depend on whether they wish to offer the legal minimum or to upgrade. An example of a 'Best Practice Maternity and Parental Policy' is set out at the end of the book showing how clear and simple a maternity policy can be if the law is simplified – this is only achievable if the terms offered are better than the legal minimum!

Most of the rights in this guide apply to employees but not to contract workers or the self-employed, unless specifically stated. Providing they satisfy qualifying conditions, such as length of service, the rights in this book apply to all employees including:

- part-time employees (no matter how many hours they work);
- employees on fixed-term contracts.

The main source of maternity rights comes from the Employment Rights Act 1996 (ERA). The most important recent changes in the law happened in 1999 when the Employment Relations Act 1999 amended ERA. The Employment Relations Act 1999 and the Maternity and Parental Leave Regulations 1999 came into force on 15 December 1999 and granted new maternity rights to employees with babies due on or after 30 April 2000, and new rights to parental leave for employees with babies due on or after 15 December 1999. These new rights are explained in this guide. However, the law changes all the time so, if in doubt, check the current position.

The law stated in this guide is correct as at **December 2000**.

ABBREVIATIONS

1999 Regulations (Regs)	**The Maternity and Parental Leave etc. Regulations 1999**
AML	**Additional maternity leave** Starts at the end of ordinary maternity leave and lasts up to 29 weeks from the start of the week of birth for employees who will have worked for one year and 11 weeks by the week the baby is due.
AWC	**Actual week of childbirth**
EAT	**Employment Appeal Tribunal**
ECJ	**European Court of Justice**
ERA	**Employment Rights Act 1996**
EWC	**Expected week of childbirth** This is the **week** in which the baby is **due**, i.e. Sunday to Saturday inclusive.
HL	**House of Lords**
HSE	**Health and Safety Executive**
HSW	**Health and Safety at Work Act 1974**
LEL	**Lower earnings limit** The lower earnings limit is the threshold for National Insurance. The LEL rate changes each year. For April 2001–April 2002, the LEL is £72. Employees who earn the equivalent of the LEL, or a little more, may not actually pay National Insurance as their contributions are zero-rated. If they earn more, their National Insurance contributions will be a percentage of their earnings.
MA	**Maternity allowance** An 18-week payment for employees who are not entitled to SMP. Paid by the Benefits Agency to those who qualify.
MATB1	The medical certificate given to a pregnant woman around the 26th week of pregnancy by her doctor or midwife which confirms the date the baby is due.

MHSWR   **Management of Health and Safety at Work Regulations 1999**

NI   **National Insurance**

OML   **Ordinary maternity leave**
18-weeks' maternity leave available to all employees regardless of length of service or hours of work.

SDA   **Sex Discrimination Act 1975**

SMP   **Statutory maternity pay**
Paid by employers to employees who satisfy the relevant qualifying conditions. SMP is made up of six weeks at 90% of the employee's average gross pay and 12 weeks at a lower fixed rate.

SSP   **Statutory sick pay**
Flat rate of sick pay paid by the employer based on National Insurance contributions in the previous eight weeks.

QW   **Qualifying week**
The qualifying week for SMP purposes is the 15th week before the EWC.

SUMMARY OF MATERNITY AND PARENTAL RIGHTS

THE RIGHT	MAIN FEATURES	WHO QUALIFIES?
Time off for antenatal care (ERA ss55–56)	Reasonable paid time off	All employees
Health and safety protection (MHSWR and ERA ss66–68)	Protection from risks before and after childbirth	All employees; must notify pregnancy in writing
Ordinary maternity leave (OML) (ERA s71, 1999 Regs 4–11)	18 weeks	All employees
Additional maternity leave (AML) (ERA s73, 1999 Regs 5–12)	Starts when OML ends and runs for 29 weeks from the AWC	Employees who have been employed for one year by the 11th week before the EWC
The contract of employment during maternity leave (1999 Regs 17)	Continues throughout maternity leave with all employment protection rights and entitlement to accrue statutory holiday under Working Time Regulations 1998	Employees on OML and AML
Contractual rights during OML (ERA s71, 1999 Regs 9)	All rights set out in the contract continue to accrue, apart from remuneration	
Contractual rights during AML (ERA s73, 1999 Regs 17)	Only the basic characteristics of the contract continue	
Redundancy during maternity leave (1999 Regs 10)	Right to be given first refusal of any suitable alternative vacancy	All employees on OML and AML

Return to work after OML (ERA s71)	Right to return to the same job	All employees
Return to work after AML (ERA s73, 1999 Regs 18)	Right to return to the same job. Only if that is not reasonably practicable may the employer offer a suitable alternative	All employees (there is a limited exception for employees in small firms with five staff or less)
Statutory maternity pay	90% of salary for six weeks, £62.20 for 12 weeks	Employees and other workers who have NI deducted at source who satisfy qualifying conditions
Maternity allowance	£62.20 a week for 18 weeks, payable by the Benefits Agency	Employed and self-employed workers who work during their pregnancy but do not qualify for SMP (because, for example, they change jobs whilst they are pregnant)
Incapacity benefit, means tested benefits	Welfare benefits for women who cannot claim SMP or MA	
Parental leave (ERA s76, 1999 Regs 13–18)	13 weeks for each parent per child born or adopted on or after 15 December 1999	Employees with responsibility for a child who have been employed for one year
Time off for dependants (ERA s57A)	Time off for dealing with emergencies	All employees

CHAPTER 1

Introduction to the law

1.1 MAIN SOURCES OF MATERNITY AND PARENTAL RIGHTS

There are two main sources of law – legislation and case law – that contain the rules on maternity and parental rights:

1. **Legislation** – Acts of Parliament (Statutes) and Regulations which set out an employee's statutory rights. The main pieces of legislation which contain most of the provisions on maternity and parental rights are the Employment Rights Act 1996 (ERA) and the Maternity and Parental Leave etc. Regulations 1999 (1999 Regulations). The 1999 Regulations are printed in full at Appendix A. Other relevant legislation is the Sex Discrimination Act 1975 and the Social Security Contributions and Benefits Act 1992.

2. **Case law** – employment tribunals, the Employment Appeal Tribunal, Court of Appeal, House of Lords and European Court of Justice regularly decide cases that interpret statute. Case decisions often lead to changes in the understanding of the law. Some areas of maternity rights law are genuinely unclear. There is not always a right answer to a question. Ultimately, an Employment Tribunal can interpret the law and reach a decision when there is a dispute.

Areas of the law most relevant to maternity and parental rights

There are four main areas of law which are most relevant to maternity and parental rights:

1. **Sex discrimination** – whatever maternity rights or obligations an employee is said to have under statute or contract, there is an overriding right not to be discriminated against. Most pregnancy or maternity-related unfair dismissal claims will also include a claim for sex discrimination.

2. **Employment protection rights** – an employee who is pregnant or on maternity or parental leave also has the benefit of general employment rights such as protection against unfair dismissal or unfair selection for redundancy and the right to paid holiday under the Working Time Regulations 1998.

3. **Statutory maternity rights** – Acts of Parliament and Regulations that set out the 'statutory minimum' entitlement.

4. **Contractual maternity rights** – Employers and employees remain free to negotiate and agree more favourable arrangements on a voluntary or 'contractual' basis. Some employers offer more favourable terms and conditions of employment than the statutory minimum such as a longer period of maternity leave or more generous pay. If a contract of employment claims to give an employee less than the legal minimum entitlement, it is unlawful. Where an employee has a contractual right as well as a statutory right, she may take advantage of whichever is more favourable to her.

The table below shows the four main areas of law that apply.

SEX DISCRIMINATION	EMPLOYMENT PROTECTION RIGHTS	STATUTORY MATERNITY RIGHTS	CONTRACTUAL MATERNITY RIGHTS
Employees who are pregnant or on maternity leave have strong protection against discriminatory dismissal and other less favourable treatment.	Employees who are pregnant or on maternity or parental leave will continue to have most of the same rights and protection as other employees, e.g. statutory holiday.	Various Acts of Parliament and Regulations set out rights to maternity leave and pay and parental leave, etc.	An employee's contract may give better rights than the legal minimum. An employer cannot give worse than the law allows.
Legislation	**Legislation**	**Legislation**	
• Equal Pay Act 1970	• Employment Rights Act 1996	• Social Security Contributions and Benefits Act 1992	
• Equal Pay Directive 1974	• Working Time Regulations 1998 SI/1998/3372.	• Maternity Allowance and Statutory Maternity Pay Regulations 1994 (as amended), SI/1994/1230	
• Sex Discrimination Act 1975	• Part-time Workers (Prevention of Less Favourable Treatment) Regulations 2000 SI/2000/1551.	• Employment Rights Act 1996	
• Equal Treatment Directive 1976		• Maternity and Parental Leave etc. Regulations 1999, SI/1999/3242.	
• Pregnant Workers' Directive 1992		• Management of Health and Safety at Work Regulations 1999 SI/1999/3242.	
• Treaty of Rome, Article 141 (right to equal pay for men and women)		• Social Security (Maternity Allowance) (Earnings) Regulations 2000, SI/2000/688	

1.2 EMPLOYEES AND OTHER WORKERS

Definition of an employee

Most of the maternity and parental rights described in this guide apply to employees only. Unfortunately, there is no single test which can be used to discover who is an employee and who is not. The ERA defines an employee as someone who works under a contract of employment (ERA s230). A contract of employment means a contract of service or apprenticeship which can be oral or in writing. It is certainly not the case that labelling someone as 'self-employed' will always be correct. In the event of a dispute, an 'employee' can make a complaint to an employment tribunal for a decision on their employment status. The tribunal would look at the factual situation, not the label attached.

Generally speaking, a worker is likely to be considered to be an employee if their employer:

- deducts tax and National Insurance from their pay; and/or
- controls the work they do, when and how they do it; and/or
- provides all the equipment for their work; and/or
- would discipline them if they did not attend work on a particular day.

Other workers

'Contract workers' such as agency workers, 'temp workers' or 'casual workers' may or may not meet the definition of 'employee'. If they are an employee, they will be entitled to the rights and benefits of all employees. If they are not employees, they still have some rights which will be dealt with in the relevant chapters, such as a right to receive statutory maternity pay if they satisfy the qualifying conditions (see 'Statutory maternity pay', Chapter 4).

The table below shows who is entitled to claim what.

Employment status	Entitled to maternity rights, e.g. maternity leave, etc.	Entitled to statutory maternity pay (if eligible*)	Entitled to protection against sex discrimination
Employee	Yes	Yes	Yes
Employee on fixed-term contract	Yes	Yes	Yes
Contract worker, e.g. casual/temporary worker, agency temp, bank nurse, etc. (unless classed as an employee)	No	Yes	Yes
Self-employed	No	No	Yes

* Women who are not entitled to SMP, or who do not meet the qualifying conditions for SMP, may be able to claim maternity allowance from the Benefits Agency.

1.3   SEX DISCRIMINATION

Sex Discrimination

Under UK and European law it is unlawful for an employer to discriminate directly or indirectly against a worker on the grounds of his or her sex. This applies to dismissal, redundancy, selection of job applicants, promotion, transfer and provision of contractual terms and conditions of work.

It is automatic direct sex discrimination to treat an employee unfavourably for reasons connected to her pregnancy or maternity leave, for example, dismissal after a period of pregnancy-related illness or demotion on return from maternity leave.

Sex discrimination law has had a significant influence on maternity and parental rights. Before going on to the detailed rules on maternity leave and pay it is important to understand the overriding protection against sex discrimination which is given to nearly all workers (including casual and temporary workers and the self-employed).

Job applicants

Job applicants are protected against sex discrimination (SDA s6). It is sex discrimination to refuse to appoint a job applicant or to withdraw a job offer because of pregnancy. An employer can ask interviewees about childcare or family plans if it is relevant to the job and all job applicants are asked the same questions. However, such questions might be seen as evidence of discrimination by an employment tribunal. Employers should take steps to reassure prospective applicants and interviewees that they will not be discriminated against on the grounds of pregnancy, childbirth or childcare responsibilities.

Self-employed and contract workers

Sex discrimination legislation covers all those who do work for another under a 'contract of services' which includes self-employed, casual and agency workers. Discriminatory treatment of such a worker could include:

- refusing to renew a contract because she is pregnant;

- refusing to give her work after the birth of her baby (despite the fact that she was not entitled to maternity leave) when a male contract worker would have been given work after a similar period of absence;

- refusing to allow an agency worker to return to her old job after the birth of her baby because she had been replaced by a permanent member of staff during her absence (*Patefield* v. *Belfast City Council* [2000] IRLR 664, NICA).

Direct sex discrimination

Direct sex discrimination arises when a woman is treated less favourably on the grounds of sex. In order to prove less favourable treatment an employee would normally have to refer to a comparator of the opposite sex who was in the same or similar circumstances. For example, if an employer refuses to employ a woman because she might have childcare responsibilities but employs a man instead.

Automatic direct sex discrimination during pregnancy and maternity leave

A period of 'Protected Status' applies during pregnancy and maternity leave when it is not necessary to show less favourable treatment than a male comparator in order to prove sex discrimination. If an employee is treated unfavourably because of pregnancy or maternity, she does not have to refer to a male comparator (because men cannot get pregnant) in order to show less favourable treatment, but can claim automatic sex discrimination. If she can show that she has suffered a detriment as a result of her pregnancy or the fact that she has been on maternity leave, e.g. dismissal or demotion, it is automatic direct sex discrimination, (*Dekker* [1991] IRLR 27 and *Webb* [1993] IRLR 27, HL & [1994] IRLR 482, ECJ).

Discrimination on grounds of pregnancy

The following cases are examples of pregnancy-related discrimination:

- Dismissal of a religious education teacher after becoming pregnant by the parish priest (*O'Neill* v. *Governors of St Thomas More RCVA Upper School and Bedfordshire CC* [1996] IRLR 372, EAT).

- Failure to appoint a woman applying for a job because she is pregnant.

- Dismissal for pregnancy-related sickness absence even if an employee with a similar length of sickness absence would be dismissed under the employer's normal sickness policy (*Brown* v. *Rentokil* [1998] IRLR 445, ECJ). Protected status exists during pregnancy so that it is automatic sex discrimination to dismiss a woman for pregnancy-related sickness. This means that **sick leave for a pregnancy-related reason should be recorded separately from other sickness absence and should not count towards a decision to dismiss.**

- Failure to pay the same sick pay as usual to a woman who is off sick for a pregnancy-related illness. The employer's ordinary sick pay policy applies during pregnancy (*Pedersen* [1999] IRLR 55, ECJ). See 'Sickness absence during pregnancy', Chapter 2.

Discrimination on the grounds of maternity leave

An employer must not treat a woman on maternity leave in a way that will affect her long-term career. The following cases are examples of maternity-related discrimination:

- Failure to consult an employee being made redundant whilst on maternity leave (*McGuigan* v. *T.G. Baynes,* unreported).

- Dismissal of an employee on maternity leave because her locum was more efficient (*Rees* v. *Apollo Watch Repairs plc* (1996) Times, 26 February, EAT).

- Deciding to make an employee redundant because her absence on maternity leave showed that she was not needed at work.

- Failure to offer an employee a performance appraisal because she was on maternity leave (*Thibault* [1998] IRLR 399, ECJ). An appraisal should be based on the time she was in the workplace.

- Failure to offer coaching for promotion.

- Failure to pay a discretionary loyalty bonus to employees on maternity leave was automatic sex discrimination (*Gus Home Shopping Ltd* v. *Green & McLaughlin* EAT, 27.9.00 (994/99)). An employee is entitled to at least the proportion of bonus earned whilst at work (*Lewen* v. *Denda* [2000] IRLR 67). This would apply to bonuses such as performance-related or profit-related bonuses.

Cases where there is no sex discrimination

It is not sex discrimination to:

- Refuse to pay full pay during maternity leave (*Gillespie* [1996] IRLR 214). See *Rights during maternity leave Chapter 5.*

- Refuse to pay maternity pay to an employee who does not qualify under the maternity pay regulations, but it *is* discriminatory not to pay at least the equivalent of what fathers receive on paid paternity leave (*Banks* v. *Tesco Stores Ltd and Secretary of State for Social Security* [2000] ICR).

- Refuse some of an employee's contractual rights during additional maternity leave, such as the right to contractual holiday (as opposed to statutory holiday which is not affected by maternity leave) (*Boyle* v. *EOC* [1998] IRLR 717).

Indirect sex discrimination

> Indirect sex discrimination arises when an employer imposes a requirement or condition on all its employees, e.g. to work full-time, which has a disproportionate and adverse impact on one sex, and the requirement (to work full-time) cannot be objectively justified.
>
> Employees must have a good reason for asking to work different hours and employers must have a good business reason to justify refusing an employee's request to work different hours in order to look after her children. See 'Requests to return to work on different hours', Chapter 6.

Section 1(b) of Sex Discrimination Act 1975 says that a person discriminates against a woman if:

> he applies to her a requirement or condition which applies or would apply equally to a man (e.g. to work full time or to work flexible shifts) but –
>
> (i) which is such that the proportion of women who can comply with it is considerably smaller than the proportion of men who can comply with it (e.g. 95% of men can work full time but statistics show that only 55% of women can do so), and
>
> (ii) which he cannot show to be justifiable irrespective of the sex of the person to whom it is applied (e.g. because the job would suit a job-share arrangement), and
>
> (iii) which is to her detriment because she cannot comply with it (e.g. because she can only find childcare for three days a week or can only find childcare until 6 p.m. each night).

Examples of indirect sex discrimination cases include:

- Requiring employees of certain grades to serve in any part of the country under a mobility clause in the contract. This requirement was found to be indirect sex discrimination as more women than men are secondary earners in the family and cannot comply with a requirement to move to a different area (*Meade-Hill* v. *British Council* [1995] IRLR 478).

- Restricting legal rights of part-timers (*R.* v. *Sec of State for Employment* ex parte *EOC* [1994] IRLR 176). Less favourable treatment of part-time employees could also now be in breach of the Part-time Workers (Prevention of Less Favourable Treatment) Regulations 2000. See 'Requests to return to work on different hours', Chapter 6.

- If an employer cannot justify a refusal to allow a woman to return to work on reduced or flexible hours after having a baby, she may have a claim for indirect sex discrimination. See 'Requests to return to work on different hours', Chapter 6, for law and practice on dealing with requests to work reduced hours, jobshare, etc.

Legal action

Claims of sex discrimination are made in an employment tribunal. The complaint must be made within three months of the act of discrimination. A tribunal can extend the time limit if it is just and equitable to do so. For example, the employee was too ill to make a claim or was waiting for her employer to take some action. There is a questionnaire procedure that claimants can use in sex discrimination cases to ask their employer for more information about their complaint and reasons for the treatment they received (SDA s74). The questionnaire must be sent to the employer within three months of the date of alleged discrimination or within 21 days of the date the complaint was received by the employment tribunal.

Compensation for sex discrimination claims is not capped. The employment tribunal can award an amount that it considers 'just and equitable'. The majority of the award will be intended to reflect lost earnings and this will be reduced if a woman has not made a real effort to find other work. There will also be an award for injury to feelings, which could be anything from about £2,000 to more than £5,000. Interest is payable on a sex discrimination award.

1.4 UNFAIR DISMISSAL AND DETRIMENTAL TREATMENT

Automatic unfair dismissal

Regardless of an employee's length of service it is unfair dismissal to dismiss her or select her for redundancy for reasons connected with pregnancy, maternity or parental leave. Dismissals for pregnancy and maternity-related reasons are automatically unfair and an employer cannot justify it as being fair and reasonable in the circumstances.

Ordinary unfair dismissal

Employees with one year's service have wider protection against being unfairly dismissed. In 'ordinary' unfair dismissal claims an employer can argue that the dismissal was fair if they can show that the dismissal was for a reason recognised by the law as potentially fair and that it was reasonable in the circumstances.

Protection from detriment

Regardless of length of service, an employee has the right not to be treated unfairly for reasons connected with pregnancy, maternity and parental leave.

Automatic unfair dismissal

Employees are given automatic protection against dismissal for reasons connected with pregnancy, maternity and parental leave. Regardless of how long an employee has been employed, it will be *automatically unfair* if she is dismissed for a reason connected with:

- her pregnancy;

- the fact that she has given birth to a child;

- the fact that she is suspended on health and safety grounds;

- the fact that s/he took or sought to take maternity leave, parental leave or time off for dependants (ERA s99 and the 1999 Regulations, Reg. 20).

An employee will also be unfairly dismissed if s/he is made redundant and the reason s/he was selected for redundancy was one set out in the list above (1999

Regulations, Reg. 20(2)). Also, if an employee is made redundant during maternity leave and is not offered any alternative employment that is available, she will have been unfairly dismissed (1999 Regulations, Reg. 20(1)(b)). See 'Redundancy', Chapter 5.

This protection applies no matter how long the employee has worked for her employer or how many hours a week she works

The law does not allow the employer to justify the dismissal as being potentially fair and reasonable, which is why it is said that a dismissal on any of these grounds is automatically unfair. Dismissal or redundancy on pregnancy or maternity-related grounds is also likely to amount to automatic sex discrimination.

Ordinary unfair dismissal

If an employee has been employed for a year when she is dismissed, she may also have a claim for 'ordinary' unfair dismissal under the Employment Rights Act 1996 (ERA s98) if the dismissal is not for a reason that is recognised as being potentially fair by the Act, or if the dismissal is carried out in an unfair way. It is potentially fair under ERA for an employer to dismiss an employee on the grounds of incapability, misconduct, redundancy, where the employee is prohibited by law from working and for some other substantial reason. The dismissal must be carried out in a fair and reasonable way. For example, failing to consult and apply fair criteria when making an employee redundant would be unfair.

Written statement of reasons for dismissal

If an employee is dismissed while she is pregnant or during her maternity leave her employer must give her a written statement of the reasons for dismissal (ERA s92(4)). An employer must provide a written statement of reasons regardless of whether the employee requests it and regardless of her length of service. An employee can make a complaint to an employment tribunal if her employer does not provide a written statement or if she believes the statement is inadequate or untrue.

Notice and notice pay

When an employer gives notice to terminate the contract, the employee is entitled to statutory notice pay of one week's notice after a month's service, plus a further week for every year of employment up to a maximum of 12 weeks (ERA s86). This does not apply where the contract requires the employer to give a period of notice which is at least one week longer than the statutory minimum and, in such cases, the employee's contractual rights apply. As notice pay is 'remuneration', it is not payable during maternity leave unless offered by the employer (see 'Rights during maternity leave', Chapter 5). If maternity pay is paid during the notice period, it can be offset against the notice pay.

Legal action

An employee can make a complaint of unfair dismissal or unfair selection for redundancy in an employment tribunal. The claim must be made within three months. A late claim may be allowed by the tribunal if it was not reasonably practicable to bring a claim within three months. The employment tribunal can award an amount that it considers appropriate to reflect loss of earnings, up to a limit of £50,000. Compensation will be reduced if the employee has not made a real effort to find other work following her dismissal or redundancy, or if the employee contributed to her dismissal in any way (excluding pregnancy or maternity reasons).

Resignation

'Dismissal' includes a situation where an employee is forced to resign because of the way she is being treated. This is called 'constructive dismissal' (ERA s95). An employee would have to show that there was a breach of contract and that her treatment amounted to being dismissed.

Protection from detriment

An employee has the right not to suffer unfair treatment at work once she tells her employer she is pregnant until the end of her maternity leave. This protection applies regardless of length of service. An employee must not be treated detrimentally for reasons connected with pregnancy, childbirth or maternity leave. This protection also applies to employees who take parental leave or take emergency time off to care for dependants (1999 Regulations, Reg. 19).

Legal Action

An employee who believes she has been unfairly treated at work can make a complaint to an employment tribunal within three months. The tribunal can award compensation that it considers 'just and equitable'. A late claim may be allowed by the tribunal if it was not reasonably practicable to bring the claim within three months.

The table below summarises the application of sex discrimination and unfair dismissal law.

Legal action	During pregnancy	During maternity leave	After maternity leave has ended	Reasons relating to parental leave or time off for dependants
s99: 'automatic' unfair dismissal	✓	✓		✓
s98: 'ordinary' unfair dismissal	✓	✓	✓	✓
s92: automatically entitled to written reasons	✓	✓		
s47C: detrimental treatment	✓ (s48)	✓	✓	✓
Breach of contract: notice pay	✓	✓ (s86–91)	✓	
Automatic sex discrimination: 'protected status'	✓	✓		
Sex discrimination: male comparator needed			✓	

CHAPTER 2

Pregnancy

2.1 HEALTH AND SAFETY DURING PREGNANCY

These rights apply to all employees who are pregnant, who are breastfeeding or who have given birth (including stillbirth) within the last six months.

An employer must take the following steps to protect the health and safety of their employees.

STEP 1   If they employ any women of childbearing age, they must carry out a 'risk assessment' of any processes, working conditions or agents which could jeopardise the health or safety of their employees or that of their babies.

STEP 2   If a significant risk is found, they must do all that is reasonable to remove it or prevent exposure to it.

STEP 3   They must give information to their employees on the risk and what action has been taken.

STEP 4   If the risk remains, they must temporarily alter the employee's working conditions or hours of work, if this is reasonable and if this avoids the risk.

STEP 5   If the risk cannot be avoided, they must offer her suitable alternative work (on terms and conditions which are not substantially less favourable than her original job).

STEP 6   If there is no suitable alternative work available, they must suspend her on full pay (i.e. give her paid leave) for as long as is necessary to avoid the risk.

Health and safety duties

Employers are obliged to take steps to protect the health and safety of all workers in their workplace (steps 1–3) (Management of Health and Safety at Work Regulations 1999, Reg. 3). There is special protection (steps 4–6) for pregnant employees and employees who have given birth in the last six months (Management of Health and Safety at Work Regulations 1999, Reg. 16). An employer must make sure that an employee's working conditions will not put her health or her baby's health at risk.

An employer's special duty under steps 4–6 arises once an employee has told her employer **in writing** that she is pregnant or breastfeeding or that she has given birth in the last six months. An employer may ask **in writing** for a certificate from her doctor or midwife for confirmation of her pregnancy (Management of Health and Safety at Work Regulations 1999, Reg. 18).

The six steps

Step 1:   Carry out a risk assessment

The employer must carry out a risk assessment when:

- there are women of child-bearing age in their workforce; and

- the work the employee does is of a kind which could involve risk, because of her condition, to the health and safety of a new or expectant mother, or to that of her baby.

This involves an assessment of the nature, degree and duration of exposure to risk from working conditions and physical, chemical and biological agents. The assessment must be recorded if the employer has five or more employees.

Common risks include:

- shocks, vibration or movement;

- handling of loads entailing risks;

- radiation;

- extremes of heat or cold;

- movements and postures;

- travelling;

- mental and physical fatigue and other physical burdens.

The assessment must be reviewed and appropriate changes made where there is a material change in the workplace environment. A woman may be vulnerable to different risks as her pregnancy progresses.

Step 2:   Take preventive or protective measures

If there is a **significant risk**, the employer must take preventive or protective measures to avoid the risk. For example, with manual handling the Manual Handling Operations Regulations 1992 require measures to protect pregnant women or new mothers carrying out certain work. There are some absolute prohibitions, for example, work involving:

- exposure to rubella virus;

- exposure to lead;

- underground mining work.

Step 3:   Give information to employees

Employees must be informed of any risks that have been revealed by the risk assessment and what action will be taken to avoid them.

Step 4:   Alter working conditions or hours of work

If it is reasonable and avoids the risk, the employer must temporarily alter an employee's working conditions or hours of work – her terms and conditions of employment must be maintained.

Step 5:   Offer suitable alternative work

If it is not possible to avoid the risk, the employer must offer suitable alternative work. The work must be:

- suitable in relation to the employee and appropriate for her to do in the circumstances; and

- on not substantially less favourable terms and conditions, taking account of status, pay, working conditions, hours of work, location, travelling time to work. The work will not be 'suitable' if the level of pay is different. The employee should be able to continue doing this work until she goes on maternity leave (ERA 1996, s67).

Step 6:   Duty to suspend on full pay

If it is not possible to avoid the risk by altering working conditions or hours of work and there is no suitable alternative work, the employer must suspend the employee from work for so long as is necessary to avoid the risk.

While suspended, an employee is entitled to be paid as though she were working – provided she has not refused suitable alternative work. Her pay is based on what she would have received if she had been working normally (even if the job she is now doing is not usually paid at her normal rate). If the employee refuses suitable alternative work, she will forfeit her right to be paid while she is suspended (ERA 1996, ss66 and 68).

An employee suspended on full pay is likely to have to start her maternity leave six weeks before the EWC as she will be absent because of her pregnancy (see 'Ordinary maternity leave', Chapter 3).

Night work

A pregnant employee doing night work must be offered suitable alternative work or suspended on full pay if she gets a doctor's or midwife's certificate stating that is necessary for her health and safety to avoid such work (Management of Health and Safety at Work Regulations 1999, Reg. 17).

Facilities to rest

The employer is obliged by law to provide 'suitable facilities' for a pregnant employee to 'rest'. These provisions are contained in the Workplace (Health, Safety and Welfare) Regulations 1992. The Regulations do not say what the suitable facilities should include, but the Code of Practice states that they should include the facility to lie down.

Compulsory leave after the birth

- There is a prohibition on an employee working within two weeks of the birth.

- There is a prohibition on women working in a factory within four weeks of the birth.

- Maternity leave is extended where necessary to provide for this (see 'Compulsory maternity leave', Chapter 3).

Job applicants

It would be unlawful sex discrimination to refuse to appoint a pregnant woman or to withdraw a job offer because she could not do the job during her pregnancy for health and safety reasons (*Mahlburg* v. *Land Mecklenburg-Vorpommern* ECJ 3.2.00 (C-207/98)).

Enforcement bodies

The Health and Safety Executive (HSE) and the Local Authority Environmental Health Department are the enforcing agencies (the size of the workplace and the level of risk to health and safety will determine which one is appropriate). With low-risk workplaces, such as retail, the Environmental Health Department is the enforcement authority. With high-risk workplaces, for example, a chemical factory, the HSE is the enforcement authority. The telephone number of the local HSE office and Environmental Health department is in the local phone book. The HSE Information Line number is: 0541 545 500.

Enforcement of the Health and Safety at Work Act 1974 (HSW)

Local authority and HSE Inspectors are given wide-ranging powers under this Act. These relate to the right of entry to premises; making examinations and investigations (including risk assessments); taking measurements, photographs and samples; the production and inspection of books and documents; the provision of facilities and assistance; questioning people; and the rendering harmless of articles and substances. Inspectors also have the power to issue improvement and prohibition notices to employers.

Under Section 33 of the Health and Safety at Work Act 1974, it is an offence for any person or corporate body to contravene any provisions of the Act. Offences are either tried in the Magistrates' Court or the Crown Court. The maximum penalty on conviction in the Magistrates' Court is set at £5,000 for most offences. Conviction in the Crown Court can lead to an unlimited fine and/or, in respect of certain offences (including failure to comply with a prohibition or improvement notice), up to two years' imprisonment.

Legal action

- An employee may make a complaint to an employment tribunal if she has not been offered alternative work before being suspended (ERA 1996, s67) or if she has not been paid whilst on suspension (ERA 1996, s68).

- An employee can make a claim for unauthorised deduction from wages if she has not been paid her full pay as a result of doing alternative work or suspension on health and safety grounds (ERA 1996, s23).

- A failure to do a risk assessment may amount to sex discrimination (*Day* v. *T Pickles Farms* [1999] IRLR 217).

- An employee may make a complaint of unfair dismissal if she has been dismissed for asserting a statutory right (ERA 1996, s104) or has been dismissed or has not been appointed because she cannot do the work due to a health and safety risk during pregnancy, breastfeeding or within six months of childbirth (ERA 1996, ss99 and 100). (See 'Unfair dismissal', Chapter 1.)

The table below summarises the law on health and safety.

Legal action	During pregnancy	During maternity leave	After maternity leave has ended
s67: right to alternative work before health and safety suspension	✓ (s70)		✓ (s70)
s68: right to pay during health and safety suspension	✓ (s70)		✓ (s70)
s23: protection of wages	✓		✓
ss99/100: automatic unfair dismissal (on grounds of health and safety	✓	✓	✓
Sex discrimination for health and safety reason relating to maternity	✓	✓	✓

Suggested clauses for a Maternity and Parental Rights Policy

Health and safety during pregnancy, breastfeeding or within six months of childbirth

Legal minimum clause	Best practice options
Once you have notified [...employer...] in writing that you are pregnant (see 'Telling your employer you are pregnant'), breastfeeding or have given birth recently (see 'Postnatal and breastfeeding health and safety'), [...employer...] will take the following steps to protect your health and safety:	
STEP 1 Carry out a 'risk assessment' of any processes, working conditions or agents which could jeopardise your health or safety or that of your baby.	
STEP 2 If a significant risk is found, do all that is reasonable to remove it or prevent exposure to it.	
STEP 3 Give information on the risk and what action has been taken.	
STEP 4 If the risk remains, temporarily alter your working conditions or hours of work, if this is reasonable and if this avoids the risk.	
STEP 5 If the risk cannot be avoided, offer you suitable alternative work (on terms and conditions which are not substantially less favourable than your original job).	
STEP 6 If there is no suitable alternative work available, you will be suspended on full pay for as long as is necessary to avoid the risk.	

2.2 ANTENATAL CARE

> An employee is entitled not to be unreasonably refused paid time off during working hours for antenatal care. For any appointment apart from the first, an employer can ask her for a doctor, midwife, or health visitor's certificate confirming that she is pregnant and written proof of the appointment.

Time off work

All pregnant employees are entitled to time off during work hours to attend antenatal appointments regardless of the hours they work and however recently they started their job. This means that an employee can take time off for her antenatal appointments, including time needed to travel to her clinic or GP, without loss of pay.

The employee should let her employer know when she needs time off and how long she is likely to be away. For appointments after the first one, her employer can ask to see her appointment card and a certificate signed by her GP, midwife or health visitor, confirming that she is pregnant.

Most antenatal appointments have to be made during the working day. Employees have the right not to be unreasonably refused any time off during work hours for antenatal care (ERA s55–56). An employer may ask the employee to arrange appointments in such a way as to minimise disruption at work but may not refuse the right to go on an appointment without good reason.

The scope of antenatal care

The law does not define the scope of 'antenatal care'. Government guidance, however, says that the definition of antenatal care 'can include parentcraft and relaxation classes' (*Maternity rights: a guide for employers and employees*, URN 99/1191). An employee will have a claim to time off for these classes if she produces a letter from her GP, midwife or health visitor which states that these classes are part of her antenatal care. Again, she should try to minimise disruption at work, which may mean going to a class outside working hours.

Payment during time off

An employee should be paid at her normal hourly rate of pay. If working hours vary from week to week, they should be averaged over the previous 12 working weeks.

Legal action

- An employee may make a complaint in an employment tribunal if she has been unreasonably refused time off for antenatal care (ERA 1996, s56) or is dismissed or selected for redundancy solely or mainly because of pregnancy (ERA 1996, s99) or for asserting a statutory right to time off for antenatal care (ERA 1996, s104). An employee can also claim recovery of loss of normal pay during time off for antenatal care (ERA 1996, s55).

Possible claim	During pregnancy	During maternity leave	After maternity leave has ended
s99: 'automatic' unfair dismissal	✓		
s47C: detrimental treatment	✓ (s48)		
s56: refusal of time off for antenatal care	✓ (s57)		
s55: refusal of paid time off	✓ (s57)		

Antenatal care

Legal minimum clauses	Best practice options
You are entitled not to be unreasonably refused paid time off during working hours for antenatal care. After the first appointment, if requested, you must produce a doctor's certificate confirming that you are pregnant and written proof of the appointment. Please try to arrange absences to minimise disruption to your work.	'Antenatal care' includes attendance at relaxation and parentcraft classes on the recommendation of your doctor or midwife. The partner of a pregnant woman is entitled to paid time off to attend antenatal appointments.

2.3   MISCARRIAGE AND STILLBIRTH

Employees whose babies are stillborn after the 24th week of pregnancy still qualify for all maternity rights.

Stillbirth

If her baby is stillborn after 24 weeks' gestation, an employee is entitled to full maternity rights and benefits. An employee whose baby is born alive but lives only a very short time (whether before or after the 24th week) is entitled to full maternity rights as this is not a stillbirth. (See 'Premature births', Chapter 3.)

Miscarriage

An employee who has a miscarriage will not be entitled to maternity rights but she will be entitled to take sick leave and must be treated in the same way as any other employee who is off sick. An employee who is dismissed because of a miscarriage may have a claim for automatic unfair dismissal (ERA s99).

Suggested clauses for a Maternity and Parental Rights Policy

Still birth

Legal minimum clauses	Best practice options
If your baby is stillborn after the 24th week of pregnancy, you still qualify for all the rights described in this policy.	

2.4 SICKNESS ABSENCE DURING PREGNANCY

Sickness during pregnancy

If an employee is off work due to sickness during pregnancy, her employer's normal sick pay policy applies. An employer must not dismiss an employee for having a pregnancy-related illness even if they would normally dismiss a sick employee in accordance with their sickness policy.

If she is off work with a pregnancy-related illness during the last six weeks of her pregnancy, an employer can start her maternity leave and pay automatically.

Pregnancy-related sickness

An employer's normal sick pay policy applies to an employee who is off sick during her pregnancy and she should notify her employer of her absence in the usual way. However, any **pregnancy-related sickness should be recorded separately** from normal sick leave as it would be automatic sex discrimination to take it into account when calculating length of sickness absence, selecting for redundancy or in a performance appraisal. Dismissal arising from pregnancy-related illness is unfair dismissal (ERA s99) and automatic sex discrimination (*Brown* v. *Rentokil Initial UK Ltd*, ECJ) (see 'Sex discrimination', Chapter 1).

The 'six week rule'

Ordinarily an employee can choose when she wishes to start her maternity leave. The earliest maternity leave can start is 11 weeks before the EWC. However, if an employee is off work with a pregnancy-related illness or pregnancy-related absence (for example, suspension on full pay on health and safety grounds) **during the last six weeks** of her pregnancy, her employer can start her maternity leave immediately (see 'Ordinary maternity leave',

Chapter 3). An employer has the discretion to ignore the odd day's pregnancy-related absence.

Statutory sick pay

If an employee is on sick leave during her pregnancy, this can affect her entitlement to statutory maternity pay (SMP). If she is in receipt of statutory sick pay (SSP) during part of her calculation period, her earnings will be below the lower earnings limit and her SMP will be reduced. If she is in receipt of SSP for the whole of her calculation period, she will lose her entitlement to SMP altogether and will have to apply for maternity allowance from the Benefits Agency (see 'Statutory maternity pay', Chapter 4).

Suggested clauses for a Maternity and Parental Rights Policy

Sickness during pregnancy

Legal minimum clauses	Best practice options
You will not be dismissed for having a pregnancy-related illness. If you are sick during pregnancy [...employer...]'s normal sick pay policy applies and you must notify [...employer...] that you are unwell in the usual way.	

CHAPTER 3

• •

Entitlement to maternity leave

3.1 ORDINARY MATERNITY LEAVE

Ordinary Maternity Leave (OML)

All employees may take 18 weeks' maternity leave.

Maternity leave cannot start earlier than the 11th week before the expected week of childbirth (EWC). It is up to the employee to choose when she starts her maternity leave, but it will start automatically if:

- **her baby is born before the start of her maternity leave; or**

- **she is absent from work wholly or partly because of pregnancy in the last six weeks of pregnancy.**

Entitlement to OML

Every employee who is employed while she is pregnant is entitled to 18 weeks' OML. It does not matter how many hours she works and how long she has worked for her employer. Part-timers, employees on fixed-term contracts and employees who have only just started working for their employer are all entitled.

Casual staff and agency workers who are not employees cannot get maternity leave but they may be entitled to maternity pay (see 'Statutory maternity pay', Chapter 4). It is sex discrimination to replace an agency worker with a permanent member of staff because she is unavailable for work due to pregnancy or childbirth (see 'Sex discrimination', Chapter 1).

The start of maternity leave

It is for the employee to decide when she wants to stop work. The earliest an employee can start her maternity leave is 11 weeks before the EWC. Maternity weeks start on a Sunday, so leave can start from the 11th Sunday before the Sunday at the start of the EWC. Maternity leave can start in the middle of a week if that is what the employee wants. She can even work right up until the day of childbirth. Her ordinary maternity leave of 18 weeks starts on the day after she stops work even if that date is in the middle of the week. Maternity pay will start on the Sunday after she stops work.

Premature births

If her baby is born alive, regardless of how premature the baby is or how short its life may be, an employee is entitled to her maternity rights. If the baby is born before the employee's maternity leave has started, her leave will start on the day of birth even if that is before the 11th week before the EWC. Employees who have premature babies have particular problems returning to work as their babies are not ready to be left when the usual period of maternity leave is over. The law does not provide for any special treatment, but some employers agree to allow an employee to extend her maternity leave or to split her leave so that she can return to work whilst the baby is in hospital and take time off when the baby comes out of hospital (which will usually be at the time the baby was originally due). However, it is probably not possible to postpone the payment of statutory maternity pay (see Chapter 4).

Absence from work in the last six weeks of pregnancy

If an employee has a pregnancy-related illness or absence (for example, suspension on health and safety grounds) **in the last six weeks of her pregnancy**, her maternity leave may be started immediately even if she is absent for only one day. An employer has the discretion not to insist that she starts her maternity leave immediately and can ignore odd days.

Preparing for maternity leave

An employer will need to consider what arrangements need to be made for covering the maternity leave period. Options may include:

*   recruiting a temporary employee (note: it is not unfair to dismiss a temporary locum who is engaged as maternity cover unless the reason for dismissal is because she is pregnant);

*   temporarily promoting an existing employee and recruiting temporary cover for their post;

*   splitting the work up amongst other employees;

*   postponing project work until the employee returns from maternity leave.

An employer should advise the employee about her rights to maternity leave and pay and the right to return to work. The employer should also advise her about the notice requirements for maternity leave and statutory maternity pay (SMP).

Notice to start maternity leave

As most employees are entitled to both maternity leave and SMP, see 'Statutory maternity pay', Chapter 4, for information on the notice required to start maternity leave and SMP. The same notice is required for employees entitled to OML as for employees entitled to AML.

An employee who is entitled to maternity leave but does not qualify for SMP is required to give her employer at least **21 days' notice of the start of her maternity leave**. Her notice should state:

- that she is pregnant;

- the expected week of childbirth (or the date of birth if her baby has been born);

- the date she intends to start her maternity leave.

An employer can ask for written notice of the date she intends to start her maternity leave (1999 Regulations, Reg. 4) and for a certificate of pregnancy, usually the MATB1.

If an employee cannot give 21 days' notice because, for example, she had to go into hospital unexpectedly, she must write to her employer as soon as is reasonably practicable with the information above. If her leave was started automatically because of pregnancy-related absence in the last six weeks of pregnancy, she must inform her employer that she is absent because of pregnancy and supply the other information set out above (apart from the date she intends to start her leave).

If notice is not given or is given incorrectly

Maternity leave will not begin until notice has been given (unless, of course, leave has started already because of birth or pregnancy-related absence). If an employee goes on leave without giving the correct notice she may be absent without leave, but it may be that it was not reasonably practicable for her to give notice.

Although an employee cannot start maternity leave until she gives notice, an employee does not risk losing her job simply because she has failed to give the correct notice.

Suggested clauses for a Maternity and Parental Rights Policy

Telling [...employer...] you are pregnant

Legal minimum clauses	Best practice options
The latest you can tell [...employer...] is 21 days before you go on maternity leave (see below). However, please tell us as soon as you feel able – until you tell us we cannot take steps to protect your health and safety. The law protects you from being dismissed or discriminated against on the grounds of pregnancy.	

Maternity leave

Legal minimum clauses	Best practice options
You may take up to 18 weeks' ordinary maternity leave (OML) regardless of your length of service or hours worked. If you have been employed continuously for at least one year and 11 weeks by the start of the expected week of childbirth (EWC), you are entitled to take additional maternity leave (AML) which begins at the end of OML and ends up to 29 weeks from the start of the week your baby is born.	All employees are entitled to [up to 11 weeks off before the EWC and up to [29] [40] [52] weeks after the birth] [up to 52 weeks leave from the start of maternity leave], regardless of length of service or hours worked. If your baby is born prematurely, before the fourth week before the EWC, [you may split your leave and return to work for a period before taking the balance of leave due to you] [you are entitled to an extra week's leave for each full week that your baby is premature].

The start of maternity leave

Legal minimum clause	Best practice options
Your leave cannot start earlier than the 11th week before the EWC. After that you are entitled to start your leave and any maternity pay you are entitled to on the date given in your notice unless:	
• your baby is born before your leave starts (in which case, your leave will start on the actual date of birth of your baby even if that is before the 11th week before the EWC); or	You need not start your leave until the birth unless you choose to start earlier.
• you are absent from work wholly or partly because of pregnancy after the beginning of the sixth week before the EWC (in which case your leave will start on the first day of pregnancy-related absence).	

3.2   COMPULSORY MATERNITY LEAVE

Compulsory maternity leave – two weeks from the birth

An employee may not return to work earlier than two weeks after the baby is born.

Suggested clauses for a Maternity and Parental Rights Policy

Compulsory maternity leave

Legal minimum clause	Best practice options
You may not return to work for two weeks after the day the baby is born.	

3.3   ADDITIONAL MATERNITY LEAVE

> **Additional maternity leave (AML)**
>
> An employee is entitled to additional maternity leave if she has been employed by the same employer continuously for at least one year and 11 weeks by the start of the EWC.
>
> AML starts at the end of OML and ends 29 weeks from the beginning of the week in which the baby is actually born.

Entitlement to AML

An employee with one year and 11 weeks' continuous employment with the same employer by the start of the EWC is eligible for this extended leave; this includes part-timers and employees who have been continuously employed on a series of fixed-term contracts.

What maternity leave and pay does she qualify for?

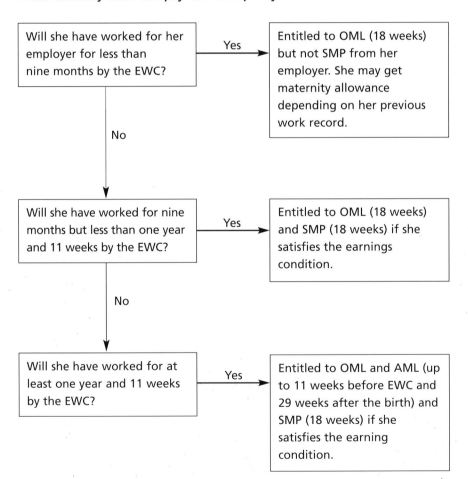

Length of service at EWC	OML (18 weeks)	AML (29 weeks)	SMP (18 weeks)	Maternity Allowance
Less than nine months	✔	✗	✗	Depends on her previous word records
More than nine months but less than one year and 11 weeks	✔	✗	✔ If she satisfies the earnings condition	✔
One year and 11 weeks	✔	✔	✔ If she satisfies the earnings condition	✔

How to calculate AML

An employee entitled to AML can take time off as follows:

- the earliest maternity leave can start is 11 weeks before the EWC. It is up to the employee when she starts her leave and she can work as near to the birth as she wishes.

- 29 weeks from the start of the actual week of childbirth (AWC). For maternity leave and pay purposes, maternity weeks always start on a Sunday. An employee may return earlier if she chooses but she must give the correct 21 days' notice.

Obviously it is impossible to say in advance exactly how long an employee will have on maternity leave as the week the baby is due to be born is not necessarily the week it will actually be born. The total length of maternity leave will depend on when she chooses to start her leave and when the baby is born. The total period could be anything from 29 weeks (in the case of an employee who takes no leave before the birth) to more than 40 weeks (in the case of a late birth where the employee has started leave 11 weeks before the EWC). It could be less than 29 weeks from the birth if an employee gives notice to return to work early.

AML starts at the end of OML

OML may begin up to 11 weeks before the week the baby is due (EWC) and will run for 18 weeks, but the 29 weeks will begin to run from the start of the week of birth (AWC). As a result, the OML period (18 weeks from the start of leave) and the 29 week period (29 weeks from the birth) will overlap. AML itself does not actually start until OML ends, although an employee entitled to AML can stay off work for 29 weeks from the AWC.

Examples

1. If the baby is born before maternity leave has started, maternity leave and pay will be as follows:

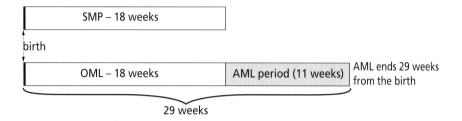

2. If the baby is born in the expected week of childbirth and the employee starts her leave four weeks before the EWC, maternity leave and pay will be as follows:

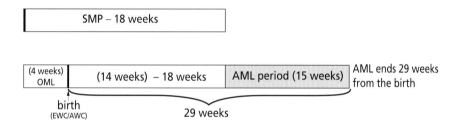

3. If the employee starts her leave four weeks before the EWC and her baby is born two weeks late, maternity leave and pay will be as follows:

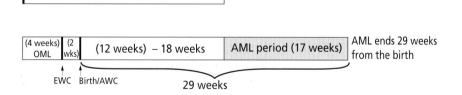

Maternity and Parental Rights – A Practical Guide

CHAPTER 4

Maternity Pay

4.1. Statutory Maternity Pay

> **Statutory Maternity Pay (SMP)**
>
> To qualify for SMP, an employee needs to:
>
> - be employed in the 15th week before her baby is due; and
>
> - have 26 weeks' continuous service at that 15th week; and
>
> - have average earnings of not less than the lower earnings limit (LEL) (£72 in 2001–2002); and
>
> - stop work because of pregnancy (unless her employment has been terminated without her consent).
>
> She is then entitled to receive SMP for up to 18 weeks at the rate of 90% of her average pay for six weeks and at the lower rate of SMP for 12 weeks (£62.20 in April 2001–2002).

Entitlement to SMP

For SMP purposes 'employees' are defined as anyone 'whose earnings attract a liability for employer's Class 1 National Insurance (NI) contributions or would if their earnings were high enough'. This includes casual staff and agency workers who have tax and NI deducted from their payslip. Employees who qualify for SMP do not actually have to pay NI, but their average earnings have to be equivalent to the LEL for NI or above (some low-earning workers are zero-rated for NI even though they earn more than the LEL).

The four-part test for SMP

1.   An employee must be employed in her job in the qualifying week which is the 15th week before the week her baby is due (EWC).

She must be employed in the qualifying week but it does not matter if she is off work sick or on holiday.

To calculate the qualifying week: find the Sunday at the start of the week in which the baby is due; count back 15 Sundays from there – this is the start of the qualifying week. The qualifying week is approximately the 26th week of pregnancy (a nine-month pregnancy is about 41 weeks). The EWC is recorded on a maternity certificate (MATB1) which is normally provided by a doctor or midwife when the employee is about 26 weeks pregnant.

2.   An employee must have 26 weeks' continuous service at the qualifying week.

She must have worked for the same employer for at least 26 weeks by the end of the qualifying week. What this means is that she must have got pregnant after starting her job. If she was already pregnant when she started, she would not have been able to work for 26 weeks by the qualifying week (roughly the 26th week of pregnancy).

3.   An employee must have average earnings of not less than the lower earnings limit in the calculation period.

Average earnings are worked out by taking pay received in the eight weeks (if she is paid weekly) or two months (if she is paid monthly) before the end of the qualifying week. This 'calculation period' is approximately weeks 18–26 of the pregnancy. The calculation period for irregularly paid employees may be different from this (see below).

The lower earnings limit for National Insurance contributions varies from year to year. For April 2001–April 2002, the LEL is £72. Confusingly, those who earn equal to or a little more than the LEL will not actually pay any NI as it is only payable on a higher rate of earnings. Therefore, an employee who pays a nil rate of NI may still get SMP.

A woman who does not earn enough in the calculation period will not qualify for SMP although she may get maternity allowance from the Benefits Agency (see below).

A woman who has a pay rise backdated into the calculation period is entitled to have that taken into account when her entitlement to SMP is assessed, but otherwise the payment is based on what a woman actually received in the calculation period. If she receives a bonus, it should be taken into account when calculating average earnings.

If a woman qualifies for SMP, her average earnings in the calculation period are then paid to her at the rate of 90% for the first six weeks of the SMP period.

How to work out average earnings in the calculation period

For employees paid weekly: add together the gross earnings from each eight weeks which fall immediately before the end of her qualifying week and divide by eight.

For employees paid monthly: add together the gross payments made on (a) the last normal monthly pay day which falls in or before the qualifying week, and after (b) the last normal pay day falling at least eight weeks before that. For most employees this means the last two monthly wage packets received by the end of the qualifying week. Once you have added the two figures together, multiply by six and divide by 52 – this will be her average weekly wage.

For employees paid irregularly: add together the gross earnings made on (a) the last normal pay day which falls in or before the qualifying week, and after (b) the last normal pay day that falls *at least* eight weeks before that (there could be quite a long gap). Count how many days there are during this period. Then divide the total salary figure by the number of days in the total period and multiply by seven to make an average week.

4. An employee must stop work for a reason connected to her pregnancy (unless her employment has been terminated without her consent).

Where an employee qualifies for SMP under the above three tests, a new rule has been introduced which applies to employees whose expected week of childbirth is on or after 4 March 2001 (The Statutory Maternity Pay (General) (Modification and Amendment) Regulations 2000). The new rule states that an employee must stop work for her employer wholly or partly because of pregnancy. Examples of reasons for stopping work because of pregnancy include, amongst other things, starting maternity leave, giving birth early, being unable to work because of a pregnancy-related illness, and for employees with more than one job, stopping one job because of tiredness due to her pregnancy (subject to an employer's health and safety duties, see 'Health and safety during pregnancy', Chapter 2).

The employer will need to check carefully all the reasons why she is stopping work. If part of the reason for stopping work is because of her pregnancy, she will still be entitled to SMP. Examples of reasons for stopping work partly because of pregnancy might include taking voluntary redundancy where it was to her advantage because of her pregnancy or resigning to take another job with lighter duties or reduced hours. (Note: a resignation caused by pregnancy could be constructive unfair dismissal, see 'Unfair dismissal', Chapter 1.)

If an employee is dismissed or her employment is otherwise ended without her consent, she will still qualify for SMP under the new rules. An employee who leaves work involuntarily for reasons wholly unconnected with her pregnancy will still be entitled to SMP. Dismissal includes redundancy, expiry of a fixed-term contract and constructive dismissal.

An employee will not qualify for SMP if she leaves her job voluntarily for a reason totally unconnected to her pregnancy after the qualifying week but before the start of maternity leave. As stated above, the employer must check carefully why she is stopping work. As these regulations are new it remains to be seen how they will be interpreted in practice.

Does she qualify for SMP? An example using rates that apply in 2001–2002

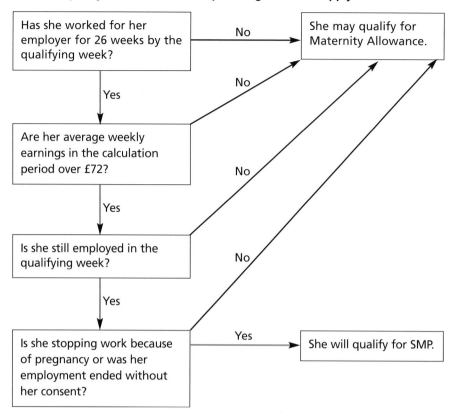

When to pay SMP

It is for the employee to decide when she wants to start her maternity leave and SMP. She can work right up until the week of childbirth if she wishes and **she will not lose SMP** (in the past, an employee lost SMP if she worked beyond the sixth week before the EWC). The only exception to this rule is that if she has a pregnancy-related illness or absence in the six weeks prior to her EWC, her maternity leave and SMP will begin automatically (see 'Ordinary maternity leave', Chapter 3). If her illness is not pregnancy-related, she can claim sick pay or statutory sick pay in the last six weeks of her pregnancy and start her maternity leave and SMP when she had planned to.

SMP is paid for up to 18 weeks and starts when an employee starts her maternity leave. The earliest leave and pay can start is the beginning of the 11th week before the EWC. This is the beginning of the Maternity Pay Period which (with rare exceptions) starts on the Sunday after a woman goes on maternity leave. If her last day of work is a Friday or Saturday, it will start immediately. If her leave starts in the middle of the week, for example, because her maternity leave is triggered by a pregnancy-related illness in the last six weeks, she may have a few days without pay until the pay period starts on the Sunday. She may get statutory sick pay in the meantime, if she qualifies.

Notice requirements to start SMP and maternity leave

An employee must give her employer at least 21 days' notice of the date she wishes to start her maternity leave. Her notice should state:

- that she is pregnant;

- the expected week of childbirth (or the date of birth if her baby has been born);

- the date she intends to start her maternity leave; and

- that she wishes her maternity pay to start.

She must also send her employer a copy of the maternity certificate (form MATB1) which her GP or midwife will give her when she is about 26 weeks' pregnant. An employer can ask her for written notice of the date she wishes to start her maternity leave.

If an employee cannot give 21 days' notice because, for example, she had to go into hospital unexpectedly, she must write to her employer as soon as is reasonably practicable with the information above. If her leave was triggered because of pregnancy-related absence in the last six weeks of pregnancy, she must inform her employer that she is absent because of pregnancy and supply the other information set out above (apart from the date her leave is due to begin). See 'Checklists and letters' at the end of this guide for examples of letters on notice requirements.

Payment of SMP

SMP is a weekly benefit. The benefit week begins on a Sunday. It will normally be paid in the same way and at the same time as the employee's wages although it may be paid in different ways if the employer chooses, e.g. a lump sum.

For the first six weeks, SMP is paid at the higher rate of 90% of the employee's average pay. After that, SMP is paid at a lower rate for up to 12 weeks. The lower rate is set by the government in April every year (£62.20 per week in April 2001–2002).

SMP is payable whether or not an employee intends to return to work. If an employee decides not to return to work after maternity leave, she cannot be asked to repay the SMP.

Employees who return to work during the maternity pay period

If an employee does any work for her employer, she cannot receive SMP for any week in which she does some work. SMP is lost at the lower rate first. For example, if an employee does three weeks' work for her employer during the 18 week maternity pay period, regardless of which weeks she works, she will receive SMP for 15 weeks and will lose the last three weeks at the lower rate. This is because SMP can only last for a period of 18 weeks and cannot be extended.

If she returns to work before the end of the 18-week SMP period and is off work sick for a week or more she will be paid SMP rather than statutory sick pay (SSP) for every complete week she is off until the end of the 18-week period. She is not entitled to SSP during the maternity pay period. She is also not entitled to SMP in any week in which she works during the maternity pay period even if it is only for a day or two. If she has no money, she should apply to the Benefits Agency for benefits.

Employees who work for more than one employer

SMP from two employers: if an employee qualifies for SMP from more than one employer, she is entitled to receive it from each of them. If the employee works before the birth for an employer who is paying her SMP, she will lose one week's SMP from that employer for each week or part-week worked. Once she returns to work after the birth, her SMP from that employer stops. She need not go back to both jobs at the same time.

Working for another employer before the birth: if she works for a new employer, or an employer who is not obliged to pay her SMP, while on maternity leave but before the birth, her entitlement to SMP is unaffected.

After the birth: if an employee starts work for a new employer, or goes back to work for another employer who employed her before the birth but after the qualifying week, she loses her entitlement to SMP from any employer who is paying it for the rest of the maternity pay period. However, if she returns to work for another employer who employed her in the qualifying week but is not obliged to pay her SMP, she will not lose her entitlement to SMP.

Employer's reimbursement of SMP

Employers can deduct an amount equal to 92% of the SMP they have paid out in the preceding period from their next payment of PAYE and NI contributions to the Inland Revenue.

Small employers, whose total gross NI liability in the last complete tax year before the qualifying week was £20,000 or less, can deduct 100% of the SMP they have paid out, plus 5% to cover any costs.

If an employee does not qualify for SMP

If the employee does not qualify for SMP, her employer should give her a form SMP1 (see below for how to order the forms) stating the reasons. She will need to show this to the Department of Social Security in order to claim maternity allowance.

Maternity Allowance

Maternity Allowance is paid by the Benefits Agency to those who have been employed or registered as self-employed for at least six months out of the last 15 months before the baby is due. She must earn at least £30 a week on average in a particular period. Maternity Allowance is paid for up to 18 weeks at a rate of £62.20 a week (April 2001–2002) or 90% of average earnings if she earns below the LEL.

Refusal or inability to pay SMP

If an employee is refused SMP, she can complain to the Inland Revenue officer based at the local National Insurance Contributions Office (within six months). It is an offence, with a fine up to £1,000, to fail to pay SMP following the formal decision of the officer. If an employer still refuses or is unable to pay SMP, the Inland Revenue may take on the liability.

An employee may also complain to an employment tribunal (within three months) that her employer has unlawfully failed to pay her wages (SMP is classified as 'wages' under the ERA 1996) (ERA 1996, s23).

Further information for employers

The Inland Revenue Helpline for employers on how pay and reclaim SMP is: 0845 7 143 143. Forms and copies of the *Inland Revenue Guide To Statutory Maternity Pay* (reference number CA29) and calculation tables (CA36) can be obtained from the Employer's Orderline: 0845 7 646 646.

Suggested clauses for a Maternity and Parental Rights Policy

Notice for start of maternity leave and pay

Legal Minimum	Best practice options
You must give a minimum of 21 days' notice before you start your maternity leave. Your notice should state:	
1) that you are pregnant;	
2) the date of your EWC (or the date of birth if this has already occurred);	
3) the date you intend to start your leave;	
4) you must enclose your MATB1;	
5) you should confirm your request for maternity pay.	
If you cannot give notice, you must make sure you give notice as soon as you reasonably can.	
You do not have to give notice in writing but it is advisable.	A letter for you to use to give notice is on page [***] of this policy.

Legal minimum clauses	Best practice options
You are entitled to receive SMP at the rate of 90% of your average pay for six weeks and a flat rate of £62.20 (from April 2001–April 2002) for up to 12 weeks if: • you have 26 weeks' continuous service at the 15th week before the EWC; and • you are still in your job in that 15th week; and • your average earnings are not below the lower earnings limit (£72 from April 2001–April 2002); and • you stop work because of pregnancy or you leave work involuntarily for reasons unconnected to your pregnancy. If you are not entitled to SMP, we will give you form SMP1 explaining why. If you have been working and earning at least £30 a week, you may qualify for maternity allowance and incapacity benefit from the Benefits Agency.	You are entitled to [[18] [26] weeks' full pay] [[10] weeks' full pay and [10] weeks' half pay] [regardless of length of service or earnings], inclusive of any SMP you are entitled to, [providing you are still employed until at least the 15th week before your EWC]. [You are entitled to the equivalent of SMP regardless of length of service or earnings, net of any maternity allowance that you can claim.]

4.2 CONTRACTUAL MATERNITY PAY

Contractual maternity pay

Maternity pay that is better than the legal minimum

The top 20% of employers pay more maternity pay than the basic legal minimum required and do not impose a requirement that average earnings are above a certain level.

Enhanced maternity pay

Maternity pay that is better than the legal minimum may be offered by the employer. Offering a longer period of leave and/or extra pay to top up SMP can be a good way of encouraging an employee to return to work, avoiding the loss of an experienced employee and the costs of recruiting and training new staff. Maternity pay should not be worse than any paternity pay offered.

Repayment of contractual maternity pay

In a case decided by the European Court of Justice, the court said that it is not sex discrimination for an employer to enforce a term in the contract requiring any additional contractual maternity pay to be repaid if an employee does not return to work after maternity leave or if an employee does not return to work for a reasonable period after maternity leave. **The SMP element of maternity pay is never repayable.** (*See* 'Not returning to work after maternity leave', Chapter 6.)

CHAPTER 5

During maternity leave

5.1   RIGHTS DURING MATERNITY LEAVE

Rights during maternity leave

- The contract of employment continues throughout ordinary and additional maternity leave (OML and AML).

- An employee continues to be entitled to her statutory rights (for example, 20 days' statutory holiday is not affected by maternity leave).

- An employee is entitled not to be discriminated against during maternity leave.

- During OML (the first 18 weeks), an employee is entitled to the benefit of her normal terms and conditions of employment – apart from her right to remuneration. For example, she can hold onto a company car.

- During AML (from the end of OML), an employee is only entitled to the benefit of some of her normal terms and conditions of employment.

Contract of employment

The contract of employment continues during maternity leave (OML and AML). A woman on maternity leave continues to be an employee and preserves her continuity of employment. If an employee has several children in quick succession, her length of service is still calculated from the start of her employment.

Statutory rights

An employee's statutory rights as an employee are not affected by her maternity leave:

- 20 days' statutory holiday a year (under the Working Time Regulations 1998). She will continue to accrue 20 days' statutory holiday a year regardless of any period of maternity leave.

- Notice of termination and, in some circumstances, notice pay (see 'Redundancy', Chapter 5, and 'Unfair dismissal', Chapter 1).

- Redundancy pay.

Sex discrimination

Because there is strong protection from sex discrimination, employers may wish to continue giving contractual benefits during AML as loss of benefits could be open to challenge under sex discrimination law. An employer must not discriminate against an employee on maternity leave by dismissing her or subjecting her to any other detriment (for example, by treating her in a way which affects her career). She should certainly be offered the same opportunities as other staff for training, career development and promotion. If a performance appraisal is due during her maternity leave, arrangements should be made to do the appraisal before she goes on leave or soon after her return. A refusal to pay a discretionary loyalty bonus because an employee is on maternity leave is automatic sex discrimination (*Gus Home Shopping Ltd* v. *Green & McLaughlin* EAT, 27.9.00 (994/99)). A refusal to pay at least the proportion of a bonus (e.g. performance-related or profit-related bonus) earned whilst at work is sex discrimination (*Lewen* v. *Denda* [2000] IRLR 67). See 'Sex discrimination', Chapter 1.

Terms and conditions during OML

During the 18-week maternity leave period, all contractual rights, such as the right to keep a company car, will continue as if the woman was still at work, apart from the right to 'remuneration', as it is expected that employees will receive maternity pay during this period.

Remuneration

During OML, an employee is not entitled to the terms of her employment which relate to 'remuneration'. The Regulations state that 'only sums payable by way of wages or salary are to be treated as remuneration'. Unfortunately, the Regulations do not define 'wages' and 'salary'. A common sense interpretation might be that wages or salary means basic pay. It is certainly arguable that remuneration does not include other monetary benefits which are usually separate terms and conditions offered to employees and are shown separately on an employee's payslip.

It is clear that the following items are not part of normal wages or salary:

- discretionary bonuses, such as a Christmas bonus;

- insurance, vouchers, club membership, reimbursement of professional subscriptions;

- participation in share schemes;

- benefits in kind such as a company car;

- pension.

It is not clear whether the following items are part of normal wages or salary:

- mortgage subsidies;

- car allowances (where a car allowance is given instead of the use of a car, it is arguable that it should still be paid during OML as employees have the right to keep a company car during OML);

- bonus or commission payments (but it would be sex discrimination to refuse to pay an employee at least the proportion of any bonus or commission that relates to the period during which she was actually at work).

Length of service

The time an employee is on OML counts towards her length of service with her employer for calculating matters such as length of service increments and redundancy.

Terms and conditions during AML

During AML, the contract of employment continues and some of its main features are preserved but the extent to which most contractual rights continue will depend on what has been agreed between employer and employee.

The employer is not obliged to continue all the rights set out in the contract but the following contractual terms continue automatically during AML:

- notice period for termination of employment;

- compensation in the event of redundancy;

- disciplinary and grievance procedures;

- implied term of trust and confidence.

An employee is still bound by the following terms:

- notice period for termination of employment;

- duty of confidentiality;

- obligation to act in good faith towards her employer;

- any terms relating to acceptance of gifts or benefits or participation in any other business (1999 Regulations, Reg. 17).

Length of service

AML counts towards length of service for statutory purposes (e.g. for statutory holiday or redundancy pay), but AML does not count towards length of service for contractual terms and conditions (e.g. pension) unless an employer agrees it. It is possible that a failure to allow length of service to accrue during AML could be sex discrimination. Any holiday over and above the statutory 20 days will have to be pro-rated to take account of the fact that any contractual holiday entitlement over and above the 20 statutory days only accrues during OML.

Legal action

If an employee is dismissed because she has had a child or is taking maternity leave, she can make a claim for automatic unfair dismissal. She also retains protection from 'ordinary' unfair dismissal during maternity leave (see 'Unfair dismissal', Chapter 1).

Suggested clauses for a Maternity and Parental Rights Policy

Rights during maternity leave

Legal minimum	Best practice options
Throughout your maternity leave:	**Throughout your maternity leave:**
• your contract of employment continues but you are not necessarily entitled to all your normal terms and conditions;	• your contract of employment continues;
• your continuity of employment is preserved so that the time you are away is not counted as a break in your employment;	• your continuity of employment is preserved so that the time you are away is not counted as a break in your employment;
• you are entitled to be considered for training, career development and promotion opportunities, etc.;	• you are entitled to be considered for training, career development and promotion opportunities, etc.;
• you are entitled to the proportion of any bonus you earned whilst at work; and	• you are entitled to the full statutory holiday of 20 days' paid leave a year;
• you are entitled to the full statutory holiday of 20 days' paid leave a year.	• you are entitled to the benefit of your normal terms and conditions of employment – apart from normal pay, for example, you may keep your company car/car allowance and holidays will continue to accrue;
During OML	
• you are entitled to the benefit of your normal terms and conditions of employment – apart from normal pay, for example, you may keep your company car/car allowance and holidays over and above the statutory minimum will continue to accrue.	• your period of maternity leave will be counted towards length of service for both your statutory and your contractual rights.

Legal minimum	Best practice options

During AML
 	
• your period of AML will not count towards length of service for contractual purposes, e.g. annual increment;
 	
• you are only entitled to the benefit of some of your normal terms and conditions of employment but the following apply:
 	
  ■ notice period for termination of employment
 	
  ■ compensation in the event of redundancy
 	
  ■ disciplinary and grievance procedures
 	
  ■ implied term of trust and confidence
 	
  ■ duty of confidentiality
 	
  ■ obligation to act in good faith
 	
  ■ any terms relating to acceptance of gifts or benefits or participation in any other business.	

5.2 PENSION CONTRIBUTIONS

> **Pension contributions**
>
> **Pension contributions at the normal rate will be paid by the employer for the first 18 weeks' leave and for any further period during which she receives maternity pay.**
>
> **If an employee pays her own contributions, they will be calculated by reference to her actual maternity pay while she is receiving it.**

Employer's contributions

The law on pensions is different from the law on other contractual rights in that it says that pension contributions (based on the employee's usual salary) must be paid by the employer during **paid** maternity leave, however long that lasts, and even if it lasts for more than 18 weeks (Social Security Act 1989, Sch. 5). SMP is paid for 18 weeks only but some employers pay contractual maternity pay for a longer period.

Even if an employee does not receive maternity pay, she is still entitled to have full pension contributions paid (based on her usual salary) during the 18-week OML period as if she was still working, as occupational pension rights continue to accrue along with other contractual rights during OML.

Whether or not occupational pension rights continue to accrue during periods of unpaid additional maternity leave will depend on the rules of the pension scheme.

Employee contributions

An employee whose pension scheme requires contributions based on a percentage of what she earns only has to pay contributions when she is receiving maternity pay. Her contribution should be based on the amount of contractual or statutory maternity pay she actually receives. She may wish to discuss with her pension provider the possibility of paying voluntary contributions to cover her unpaid maternity leave.

Suggested clauses for a Maternity and Parental Rights Policy

Pensions

Legal minimum	Best practice options
Pension contributions at the normal rate will be paid by [...employer...] for the first 18 weeks of OML and any further period during which you are receiving maternity pay.	Pension contributions at the normal rate will be paid by [...employer...] throughout your maternity leave.
If you pay your own contributions they will be calculated by reference to your actual maternity pay while you are receiving it.	
If you have any queries check your options with the pension company/personnel department.	

5.3 REDUNDANCY DURING MATERNITY LEAVE

> It would be automatic unfair dismissal and sex discrimination to select an employee for redundancy on the grounds that she is pregnant, has given birth or has taken maternity leave. The employer's normal redundancy policy applies, for example, she is entitled to be fully consulted and to be offered voluntary redundancy if others are being offered it.
>
> If an employee's post becomes redundant during her maternity leave, she is entitled to be offered first refusal of any suitable alternative vacancies which must be kept open for her return. Failure to offer suitable alternative work would be automatic unfair dismissal.
>
> If no suitable alternative exists, she will be entitled to redundancy pay.

Definition of redundancy

There are three main redundancy situations:

- when the whole business closes down either temporarily or permanently;

- when the place where the employee is employed closes down;

- when fewer employees are needed to do the work or to work in the place where they are employed (ERA 1996, s139).

An employee who is redundant is entitled to statutory redundancy pay and paid notice (ERA ss86–89) or to receive any contractual redundancy and notice pay offered by the employer (but see 'Redundancy during maternity leave' below).

Selection for redundancy

The employer must use a fair method for deciding who to make redundant. It is unfair dismissal and sex discrimination to select an employee because:

- she is pregnant;

- she is on maternity leave;

- as a result of her absence on maternity leave, her employer believes they can do without her – *Intelligent Applications* v. *Wilson* 6.10.92 (S)EAT 644/91;

- her employer has realised that the maternity replacement is a better worker – *Rees* v. *Apollo Watch Repairs* (1996) Times, 26 February, EAT (note: this is not a redundancy situation anyway);

- she has a poor sickness record because of pregnancy-related absences (see 'Sickness absence during pregnancy', Chapter 2);

- she works part-time.

Before making redundancies, an employer must use a fair procedure to decide who to make redundant. A common practice for deciding who to make redundant is 'last in first out'. However, criteria such as length of service may be indirectly sex discriminatory partly because employees who take maternity leave may appear to have had less service. A failure to consult an employee because she is absent on maternity leave may make the process unfair and discriminatory, as will a failure to involve her in the same process being applied to employees still at work.

Redundancy during maternity leave (OML and AML)

An employee who is made redundant while she is *actually on* maternity leave (OML and AML) has the right to be offered and to have first refusal of any suitable jobs available in the organisation. She takes priority over any other worker (1999 Regulations, Reg. 10). She should not have to apply for jobs or go for interviews but should be offered any suitable alternative vacancies.

Failure to offer any suitable alternative work that is available would be automatic unfair dismissal (1999 Regulations, Reg. 20).

An employee *due to go* on maternity leave has the right along with all other staff to be considered for other vacancies – failure to consider her would be sex discrimination. She should not be left out because she cannot take up a new appointment because of maternity leave.

Suitable alternative work

Any offer of alternative work must be suitable for the employee and appropriate for her to do in the circumstances. It must also be on terms and conditions as to location, pay, status, etc. that are not substantially less favourable than her old job (1999 Regulations, Reg. 10). If the employee unreasonably refuses a suitable offer, she will lose her entitlement to a redundancy payment. 'Suitability' generally refers to job-related factors such as pay, grade, hours and location. A common offer is for the same job but in a different location. It may be reasonable for her to refuse on the grounds of personal circumstances such as extra travelling time and expense, family commitments, caring responsibilities, domestic factors and health.

Redundancy pay during maternity leave (OML and AML)

If an employee is made redundant during maternity leave, she is entitled to:

1. Statutory redundancy pay or any contractual redundancy scheme.

2. Statutory or contractual notice pay – a minimum of one week's notice after a month's service, plus a further week for every year of employment over two years up to a maximum of 12 weeks (ERA ss86–89). If her contract provides for one week's notice more than her statutory entitlement, she has to rely on her contractual rights. This means that she will only be entitled to notice pay during her maternity leave if it is offered by her employer.

3. Pay for any statutory holiday accrued until her final day of employment. This has to be calculated according to a set formula under the Working Time

Regulations 1998. If she is also entitled to extra contractual leave, this will accrue over the first 18 weeks of her maternity leave and her final holiday pay should also include an element of contractual holiday.

4. Full statutory maternity pay (if she qualified for it). If an employee is dismissed or selected for redundancy in order to avoid paying her SMP, she can make a complaint to the Inland Revenue Officer at the Contributions Office. The employer is still liable to pay SMP. The liability of an insolvent employer will be met by the Inland Revenue. An employee can claim unlawful deduction of wages in an employment tribunal for unpaid SMP.

Unfair redundancy

If an employee maintains that there is no genuine redundancy situation, she will have a claim for ordinary unfair dismissal and also automatic unfair dismissal if the dismissal is pregnancy/maternity related (see 'Unfair dismissal', Chapter 1). She would also have a claim for sex discrimination.

Suggested clauses for a Maternity and Parental Rights Policy

Redundancy during and after maternity leave

Legal minimum	Best practice options
You will not be made redundant for any reason connected to the fact that you have taken maternity leave. If your post becomes redundant during your maternity leave, you are entitled to be offered any suitable alternative post that exists in the organisation.	
If no alternative exists, [...employer...]'s normal redundancy policy applies. In most cases, you will be entitled to full notice pay.	You will be entitled to the full amount of notice pay that you would normally receive.

CHAPTER 6

Return to work after maternity leave

6.1 RETURN TO WORK AFTER ORDINARY MATERNITY LEAVE

> An employee has the right to return to the same job at the end of ordinary maternity leave (OML). She does not need to give notice that she intends to return to work at the end of OML.
>
> If she wants to return to work *before* the end of OML, she must give 21 days' notice.

Return at the end of OML

An employee does not need to give any notice of return if she is going back to work at the end of her OML period (that is, 18 weeks from the actual day she began her leave). As with annual leave, no notice of return is required.

Notice of return before the end of OML

If the employee wants to return to work early, she must give her employer 21 days' notice of the date she will be returning. If she does not give 21 days' notice and just turns up at work before the end of the 18-week period, her employer can send her home and refuse to pay her for 21 days or until the end of her 18-week period, whichever is earlier (1999 Regulations, Reg. 11).

Return to the same job

When an employee returns from OML it must be to **exactly the same job**. In other words, her job must be kept open for her. If the employee decides not to return to work, she must resign in the normal way, giving the required notice.

Legal action

If the employee is not allowed to return to work, or is given a different job, she will have unfair dismissal/detrimental treatment and sex discrimination claims.

6.2 RETURN TO WORK AFTER ADDITIONAL MATERNITY LEAVE

An employee need give no notice if she returns at the end of additional maternity leave (AML). If she wants to return early, she must give her employer at least 21 days' written notice of the date of return.

An employer can write to her at any time after 15 weeks from the start of her maternity leave to ask for confirmation of the date her baby was born and whether she intends to return to work.

An employee has the right to return to the same job after AML or, only if that is not reasonably practicable, a suitable job on very similar terms and conditions.

Return at the end of AML

An employee does not need to give any notice of return if she is going back to work after her AML period (that is, 29 weeks from the start of the week her baby was actually born). An employer can calculate that an employee who is entitled to AML will be back at work at the end of the 29-week period and, as with annual leave, no notice of return is required.

Return to work early

If the employee wants to return to work early, she must give her employer 21 days' notice of the date she will be returning. If she does not give this notice and just turns up at work before the end of the AML period, her employer can send her home and refuse to pay her for 21 days or until the end of her AML period, whichever is earlier (1999 Regulations, Reg. 11).

Employer's request for confirmation of intention to return

An employer may write to an employee who is entitled to AML at any time from 15 weeks after the start of her maternity leave asking her to confirm the date her baby was born (in order to calculate the end of AML) and whether she is **intending** to return to work. She must reply in writing within 21 days or she could lose protection against detriment or dismissal for having taken maternity leave. An employer's request must be in writing and must explain how to calculate the date on which AML will end and that she will lose her right to 'automatic' protection against detriment or dismissal if she does not reply within 21 days (1999 Regulations, Reg. 12).

An employer may not write to an employee before the 15th week from the start of her maternity leave to ask if she intends to return. This means that if the employee started her maternity leave at the earliest date possible (i.e. 11 weeks before her baby was due), she may only recently have given birth or have a very young baby. In order to keep her options open, she has no alternative but to say she is intending to return at this stage. If the employee decides later on that she is unable or does not wish to return, there is no penalty. If she decides not to return, she is obliged to comply with any contractual terms relating to notice of resignation. But, informing her employer that she has decided not to return is not a resignation.

If the employer does not write, or does not warn her clearly in the letter of the consequences of failing to reply, the employee need take no action.

Return to the same job

When an employee returns from AML, she is entitled to have her old job back, unless it is not reasonably practicable for her to return to that job (1999 Regulations, Reg. 18).

Where it is not reasonably practicable for an employee to return to her old job

If it is not reasonably practicable for an employee to return to her old job after AML, she is entitled to a suitable alternative job on terms and conditions as to pay, status, job security, etc. that are **no less favourable** than her old job (1999 Regulations, Reg. 18). If an employee is not given a sufficiently similar job, she can make a claim for unfair dismissal/detrimental treatment and sex discrimination.

A 'job' is defined in terms of 'the nature of the work which the employee is employed to do under her contract, and the capacity and place in which she is employed' (1999 Regulations, Reg. 2). In practice, it is often quite difficult to know when an employee is returning to the same job, and when she is not (see cases such as *McFadden* v. *Greater Glasgow Passenger Transport Executive* [1977] IRLR 327, IT). There are not many situations where it is not reasonably practicable to allow an employee to return to the same job, or where a sufficiently similar alternative is available.

Legal action

If an employee is not allowed to return to work, or her previous job still exists and she is not allowed to return to it, she will have unfair dismissal and sex discrimination claims, or she may be redundant and entitled to redundancy pay.

Provisions for small employers for covering absence on AML

There are special provisions for small employers who employ five or fewer employees (including the number of employees employed by any associated employer) in the period immediately before the end of AML. The employer should make all reasonable efforts to cover an employee's absence in a way that allows her to return at the end of AML. But, if an employer can show that it is not reasonably practicable *either* to offer her the same job back *or* to offer her a suitable alternative on similar terms and conditions with her employer or any associated employer, she cannot claim automatic unfair dismissal (1999 Regulations, Reg. 20 (6)). If it is not reasonably practicable to allow her to return to her job but she accepts or unreasonably refuses an offer of suitable alternative work with an associated employer, she cannot claim automatic unfair dismissal (1999 Regulations, Reg. 20(7)).

She will still have an ordinary unfair dismissal and sex discrimination claim if she is dismissed without a good reason after taking maternity leave. (See 'Unfair dismissal' and 'Sex discrimination', both in Chapter 1).

Suggested clauses for a Maternity and Parental Rights Policy

Returning to work

Legal minimum	Best practice options
Returning after OML (18 weeks) You do not need to give notice that you intend to return to work. You have the right to return to exactly the same job. If you want to return to work *before* the end of your maternity leave, you must give at least 21 days' notice. **Confirmation that you intend to return to work** If you qualify for additional maternity leave, [...employer...] may write to you at any time from 15 weeks after the start of your basic maternity leave asking you to confirm the date your baby was born and that you are returning to work. You must reply in writing within 21 days. There is no penalty if you change your mind later, but you must confirm your intention to return. **Returning after AML** You do not need to give notice that you intend to return to work. If you want to return to work *before* the end of your maternity leave, you must give [...employer...] at least 21 days' notice. You have the right to return to the same job or, if that is not reasonably practicable, a suitable job on similar terms and conditions.	You do not need to give notice that you intend to return to work. If you want to return to work *before* the end of your maternity leave, you must give at least 21 days' notice. You have the right to return to exactly the same job no matter how much maternity leave or parental leave you take, provided you give any notice required. Please keep in touch with us during your maternity leave. We will keep in touch with you, too [by sending you the staff newsletter]. Please let us know when your baby has been born so that we can calculate with you the date your maternity leave ends.

6.3 SICKNESS DURING AND AFTER MATERNITY LEAVE

> **Sickness after maternity leave**
>
> If an employee is too ill to go to work after her maternity leave has ended, her employer's normal sick leave and sick pay policy applies.

Sickness during maternity leave

An employee is not entitled to contractual sick pay while she is on maternity leave, but she may be able to claim incapacity benefit from the Benefits Agency if she has paid some National Insurance contributions in the last two to three years.

Sick leave after maternity leave

As the contract of employment continues during maternity leave, an employee who is unwell and cannot go back to work once her maternity leave has ended is technically back at work but on sick leave. Her employer's normal sick leave and sick pay rules apply and she should follow any sickness procedures in place at her work. Neither the employee nor the employer can postpone a return from maternity leave because of sickness or for any other reason.

During sick leave, the employee should be paid any contractual sick pay required by the contract. It is unlikely that she will be entitled to statutory sick pay (SSP) at the end of maternity leave, as she will not have earned enough in the calculation period to qualify for SSP, but she may be entitled to incapacity benefit from the Benefits Agency.

Legal action

If an employee is dismissed because she is unwell and unable to return to work, she will probably have a claim for unfair dismissal. A dismissal which takes account of any periods of pregnancy-related sickness or the maternity leave period itself would be automatic unfair dismissal and sex discrimination. Dismissal for a pregnancy-related illness which continues or appears after maternity leave would be automatic unfair dismissal. However, dismissal for a birth-related illness after the end of maternity leave would not be automatically unfair, but may be an 'ordinary' unfair dismissal.

If the employee has worked for her employer for one year, she will have 'ordinary' unfair dismissal protection and her employer will be expected to act reasonably in dismissing her for incapability on the grounds of long-term sickness absence. For example, the employer should gather medical information about her illness, consult, consider the impact of her illness on the business, etc. An employer must always abide by the procedures for dismissal set out in a contract even if she has been employed for less than one year. A dismissal in circumstances where a man would not be sacked would also be sex discrimination.

Suggested clauses for a Maternity and Parental Rights Policy

Sickness during and after maternity leave

Legal minimum	
During maternity leave	
You are not entitled to sick pay whilst you are on maternity leave although you may be able to claim incapacity benefit from the Benefits Agency.	
After maternity leave	
Once your maternity leave has ended, if you are unwell and unable to come to work you will be on sick leave in the normal way. You must follow the procedures in [...employer...]'s sickness policy.	

6.4 NOT RETURNING TO WORK AFTER MATERNITY LEAVE

Resignation

If an employee decides not to return to work after maternity leave, she must give her employer the notice she is obliged to give under her contract. Her employer will send her a P45 and will pay her for any holiday that she has not taken including any holiday accrued whilst she has been on maternity leave.

Statutory maternity pay

An employee's entitlement to statutory maternity pay is not affected if she resigns. As long as she was employed in the 15th week before the EWC and qualifies for SMP, she will not have to repay any SMP that she receives.

Contractual maternity pay

The question as to whether any contractual maternity pay (paid on top of statutory maternity pay) must be repaid if an employee resigns depends on what the contract says. It is clear that if the contract does not require repayment (e.g. for failing to return to work or for failing to return for a certain period), there is no right to ask for repayment. However, where it does, an employee must repay and if an employer insists on repayment they can sue for debt in the County Court.

The employee can negotiate to repay the debt in instalments.

Suggested clauses for a Maternity and Parental Rights Policy

If you do not intend to return to work after maternity leave

Legal minimum	Best practice options
You must give the notice of resignation required by your contract. When you resign [...employer...] will send you your P45 and will pay you for any holiday that you have not taken including any holiday accrued whilst you have been on maternity leave.	
You will not have to repay any SMP that you have received.	You will not have to repay any contractual maternity pay received [as your maternity pay is not repayable even if you do not intend to return to work] [if you return to work for three months or more], but please let us know as soon as possible so that we can plan to recruit a replacement.

6.5   REQUESTS TO RETURN TO WORK ON DIFFERENT HOURS

> **Part-time and flexible working hours**
>
> **If, at the end of maternity leave, an employee's childcare responsibilities make it impossible for her to return to work full-time, her employer must seriously consider a request to return on a part-time or flexible basis in the short or long term.**

Right to request different working hours

If an employee needs to change the way she works after having a baby, she has the right to have a request to return to her original job on a part-time, job share or flexible basis seriously considered by her employer. Her employer must have a good reason ('justification') for refusing to let her work different hours so that she can both work and care for her children. An employer will only know whether a particular job would work on different hours by giving the matter a lot of thought. The employer and employee should look carefully at her job together and try to work out a suitable alternative work pattern. See best practice guidance on part-time work requests, below.

Once part-time work has been agreed, it is a permanent arrangement. If an employee has returned part-time, she does not have the right to go back to full-time work later, unless it has been agreed in advance or she has a right to a phased return in her contract or she has used parental leave to work part-time for a while.

Duty to consider different hours

An employer has a duty to consider all forms of working which would be compatible with the particular job in question and the needs of the employee. Different hours could include:

- **Part-time working**: this is the most common request and can involve any number of hours. Although the Labour Force Survey definition of 'part-time work' is less than 30 hours per week, it can be more where the normal weekly hours are higher, or as low as two hours a week.

- **Job sharing**: this is where one job is shared between two employees, usually on a 50/50 basis, for example, two and a half days each or mornings and afternoons. But it may be a different split, for example, two days/three days.

- **Flexible hours**: the employer has some choice over the hours worked, such as 'core' hours during which an employee must work, e.g. 11 a.m. to 3 p.m. The employee can choose which other hours to work. Some schemes allow an employee to work extra hours on some days and then take one day off every fortnight or month. Alternatively, an employee may simply want to have a short lunch break in order to arrive at work later or leave earlier.

- **School hours and/or term-time working**: this is less common and such arrangements may only be suitable in a few jobs, e.g. teaching. However, Boots the Chemists allows some employees to work term-time only.

- **Working from home some or all of the time**: modern technology has increased the possibility of many jobs being done wholly or partly from home.

- **Shift working**: allowing employees to swop shifts between themselves enables some flexibility or agreeing shifts that fit in with childcare.

The organisation New Ways to Work can offer practical advice about different working patterns (see their listing under 'Useful contacts' at the end of this guide).

Indirect sex discrimination

The Sex Discrimination Act 1975 says that it is indirectly discriminatory to refuse to allow an employee to return on different hours without a good reason if she can show that there is a requirement or condition (e.g. to work full time):

1. which a considerably smaller proportion of women than men can comply with (93% of male employees work full time; 55% of female employees work full time: Labour Force Survey, winter 95/96);

2. which is to the employee's detriment (if she has to resign because she can no longer work full time);

3. which the employer cannot justify (which means the employer must seriously consider and have good reasons for refusing).

Reasons for requesting different working hours

Legal protection only applies if an employee would be disadvantaged by not being allowed to work different hours. She must have a good reason for asking for reduced/flexible working hours, such as:

- she cannot find full-time childcare;

- she cannot afford to pay for full-time childcare;

- she has to be at home when her children come home from school, perhaps because they have special needs;

- she is suffering from severe stress from working long hours (perhaps because the father of the child cannot share the childcare).

Reasons for the employer to refuse

As flexible working has become more widespread, many of the reasons for refusing a request to work part time are no longer seen as justification by employment tribunals. For example, the following reasons have been rejected by tribunals:

- There are no part-time vacancies (a blanket policy against part-time work is likely to amount to indirect sex discrimination). An employer must look at whether the employee's original job could be done part-time or as a job share.

- The job is too senior. The law applies to all employees, no matter how senior. Many jobs, including managerial jobs are successfully done on a part time, flexible or job share basis. In *Robinson* v. *Oddbins Ltd*, a refusal to let the manageress work on a job share basis was found to be indirect sex discrimination. The tribunal decided that the manager's job could be shared between two people and that for some aspects of the job, such as the responsibility for stock control, it was even preferable to have two people performing the work. The tribunal also noted that little consideration had been given to her request.

- Last-minute overtime is an essential part of the job. The employer should consider a job share or setting up an 'on call' rota.

- It is too expensive – costs are not usually any higher for part-timers.

- Continuity is crucial. There are usually practical ways to ensure continuity, such as keeping good records and making sure that there are effective ways of communicating.

It is also arguable that a refusal of child-friendly working hours is contrary to the right to family life under Article 8 of the Human Rights Act 1998.

An employer may be justified in refusing different hours if there are good business reasons and there is no alternative solution (e.g. if particular opening hours are essential to the business and need to be covered). In *Mawkin* v. *The Cats Whisker,* a refusal of part-time work was found to be justified. The tribunal decided that in a hairdressing salon which stayed opened until 7.00 p.m. in the evenings, it would be unfair on other staff if Mrs Mawkin were to leave at 5.30 p.m. The salon had good business reasons for staying open late and it was justifiable to require staff to work some late shifts.

Alternative job offers

On return from maternity leave an employee has the right to have her old job back. If her request to work part time is refused but she is offered a different job on a part-time basis (e.g. at a lower grade) or part-time hours on worse terms and conditions (e.g. a lower hourly rate of pay) she does not have to accept it. She may have a claim for indirect sex discrimination for a refusal to allow her to continue in her old job on different hours. If she is forced to take a different job, she would have a claim for automatic unfair dismissal/ detrimental treatment and sex discrimination.

If a woman resigns as a result of the refusal to allow her to work part time, she could claim constructive unfair dismissal as well as sex discrimination.

Part-time Workers (Prevention of Less Favourable Treatment) Regulations 2000

The Part-time Workers Regulations state that part-time employees must be treated in the same way as comparable full–time employees with regard to their terms and conditions of employment. Part–time employees should receive the same level of salary and other contractual benefits as their full-time equivalents on a pro-rata basis according to the number of hours/days worked. The holiday entitlement of part timers should be pro rata that of full timers. Part timers are still entitled to 13 weeks' parental leave which should be based on their normal working week, for example, an employee who works two days a week will have 13 weeks at two days a week, i.e. 26 days' leave.

Part-time employees should not be excluded from access to benefits, such as pension schemes, profit sharing and career break schemes, unless different treatment of part-timers can be justified on objective grounds other than their part-time status. Where a benefit cannot be applied pro-rata, such as health insurance, that is not in itself objective justification for denying it to part-time employees. The less favourable treatment of part time employees must still be justified on objective grounds which might include the disproportionate cost to the organisation of providing such a benefit or where necessary to meet a real need of the organisation.

Part-timers should not be excluded from training simply because they work part time and previous or current part-time status should not be a barrier to promotion to a position whether full time or part time.

Best practice guidance on part-time work requests

Best practice guidance which was issued by the Government in conjunction with the Part-time Workers Regulations 2000, is not binding but outlines factors which should be taken into account in order to comply with the Regulations. The Guidance (published on and available from the DTI website: www.dti.gov.uk/er/pt-info.htm) suggest that:

- employers should seriously consider requests to change to part-time working or job sharing and explore how this change could be accommodated;

- employers should consider establishing a procedure for discussing with employees whether they wish to change from full-time to part-time employment for any reason;

- larger organisations should keep a database of those interested in job-sharing arrangements;

- employers should periodically review how employees are provided with information on the availability of part-time and full-time positions;

- employers should consider how to make it easier for employees to vary their hours, including transferring between part-time and full-time work, to the benefit of both employees and employers.

When considering requests to work part time the Best Practice Guidance suggests the following factors may be taken into account:

- Does someone need to be present in this post during all hours of work?

- Can the post be filled as a job share?

- Is there a suitable candidate for a job share or could one be recruited?

- Can all the necessary work be done in the hours requested?

- Can the job be redefined to make it easier to do part time?

- Is the change for a known period?

- How much would it cost to recruit and train a replacement if the worker left?

- What benefits would the organisation get from this arrangement? (e.g. more commitment, keep a valued member of staff, a better skilled worker if time is used for training or education, lower wage bill, keep staff cover for peak periods.)

- Effect on the morale and commitment of other staff.

In larger organisations, measures to help employees combine work and childcare might include considering whether it would be cost-effective to provide childcare facilities onsite, or whether a contribution towards childcare costs could be offered. Both large and small organisations might consider whether it would be appropriate to introduce flexible forms of working, such as term-time working, lunch-time working, flexi-time, home-working, parental leave scheme, career break scheme and reduced hours' working.

Suggested clauses for a Maternity and Parental Rights Policy

Return to work on a part-time and/or flexible basis

Legal minimum	Best practice options
If your childcare responsibilities make it impossible for you to return to work full time after maternity leave, [...employer...] will seriously consider your request to return to your old job on a part–time and/or flexible basis in the short or long term.	If you wish to work different hours after maternity leave, you may do so unless the new arrangement would be detrimental to the needs of the business.

6.6   POSTNATAL HEALTH AND SAFETY AND BREASTFEEDING

Health and safety after childbirth

Employees who have given birth (including stillbirth) in the last six months and those who are breastfeeding are protected under health and safety regulations.

Postnatal health and safety duties

Employers have a duty to protect the health and safety of an employee who is breastfeeding and to protect her baby's health. The employer must carry out a risk assessment and consider whether her working conditions are a risk to her health or to the health of her baby (see 'Health and safety during pregnancy', steps 1–3, Chapter 2).

Scientific evidence shows that a baby's health is put at risk if they are not breastfed. If working conditions stop an employee from breastfeeding, they are putting the baby's health at risk and this may be against the law. There are very few direct risks at work to breast milk itself, but see 'Dangerous substances' below.

It may be indirect sex discrimination to refuse a request to work different or reduced hours in order to continue breastfeeding on return to work. An employee who is penalised because she wishes to continue breastfeeding may have a claim for indirect sex discrimination.

Expressing breast milk

Breastfeeding includes expressing milk. An employee who cannot feed her baby during the day (for example, because her baby is not in a nursery close to work) can express milk into a container, either by hand or by using a small pump. This provides a supply of breast milk which can be left with the baby's carer and gives the baby the advantages of drinking only breast milk. Breastfeeding works on the principle of supply and demand. The more the baby feeds, the more breast milk is produced. If the baby does not feed, less milk will be produced. If a mother is separated from her baby she has to express milk or her milk supply will diminish and she will no longer be able to feed the baby fully. The best time to express milk is at the times the baby would normally be feeding because the mother's breasts are full, which will be during the working day.

Because babies are vulnerable to infection, the mother needs to be able to wash her hands before expressing and she needs to be able to wash and sterilise any equipment she uses. Having collected the breast milk, the mother needs to keep it refrigerated until she can take it home.

Action to avoid the risk

When there is a risk to the baby's health because breast milk is affected or breastfeeding is jeopardised, the employer should take steps to avoid the risk (see 'Health and safety during pregnancy', steps 4–6, Chapter 2) or the employer may be breaking the law. An employer can ask for confirmation in writing that the employee is breastfeeding. Steps to avoid the risk include temporarily changing an employee's working conditions or hours of work if it is reasonable and avoids the risk. For example, she should be allowed to work shorter shifts or have suitable breaks to express milk, in order to continue breastfeeding. She could also expect to have a suitable place to go in order to express milk at work, i.e. a place to rest, a place to sterilise equipment and access to a fridge in which to store milk.

If an employee's GP or health visitor advises that the job is so stressful that even with temporary adjustments her ability to breastfeed could be put at risk, the employer should consider temporary transfer to alternative work. In extreme cases, it may be necessary to suspend the employee on full pay.

Dangerous substances

Some hazardous substances such as lead can enter breast milk and might pose a risk to the breastfed baby. If the work brings an employee into contact with a dangerous substance, she must make sure her employer knows (in writing) that she is breastfeeding. If the job cannot be made safe, she must be transferred to a suitable alternative job or suspended on full pay. For advice on whether a particular substance could be a risk, consult the occupational health nurse or ring the Health and Safety Executive (020 7717 6000).

Night work

A breastfeeding employee doing night work must be offered suitable alternative work or suspended on full pay if she gets a doctor's or midwife's certificate stating that it is necessary for her health and safety (or that of her baby) to avoid such work (MOHSW 1996, Reg. 13b).

Facilities for breastfeeding or expressing

The employer is obliged by law to provide 'suitable facilities' for a breastfeeding mother to 'rest'. These provisions are contained in the Workplace (Health, Safety and Welfare) Regulations 1992. The regulations do not say what the suitable facilities should include but the Code of Practice states that they should be conveniently situated in relation to sanitary facilities and, where necessary, include the facility to lie down. New guidelines from the European Commission on the health and safety of pregnant workers who have recently given birth or are breastfeeding (COM (2000) 466) recommend that measures should include:

• access to a private room in which to breastfeed or express breast milk;

• use of secure, clean refrigerators for storing expressed breast milk whilst at work and facilities for washing, sterilising and storing receptacles;

• time off (without loss of pay or benefits and without fear of penalty) to express milk or breastfeed.

Good practice

In order to breastfeed or express milk successfully the mother needs to feel comfortable and relaxed. She needs to be in a private place where she will not be embarrassingly interrupted by a colleague. Although private, the ladies toilet is not a suitable place to breastfeed or express milk as it is an unhygienic and unpleasant environment in which to feed a baby or collect milk.

Employers could consider offering the following facilities:

• use of a room that is warm, clean and private, preferably with a lockable door (e.g. the sick room or a spare office). The room will need an electric socket if the employee is using an electric breastpump or steam steriliser;

• somewhere to wash her hands and equipment;

• somewhere clean to leave a steriliser or a bowl with sterilising solution, or use of a microwave oven if there is one;

• use of a fridge to keep bottles of expressed milk;

• a low, comfortable chair.

Ideally, a breastfeeding employee should be allowed breaks either to visit her baby or to express milk at the same time of day as she would normally feed her baby at home. Obviously, this will depend on the nature of the employee's work and in some cases an exact routine may be impossible. However, a starting point for good practice should be to talk to the employee herself about what breaks she will need for expressing or breastfeeding. Some women find expressing milk quick and easy, others may take longer. The number of breaks or the length of breaks may vary over time as the feeding pattern of babies varies according to their age, health and the individual child. It is difficult or sometimes physically impossible to breastfeed or express milk under pressure, so an employee should not feel timed. It may be necessary to ensure adequate cover during breastfeeding breaks so she is not pressurised into reducing or abandoning them.

The employee's needs as a breastfeeding mother should be taken into account when scheduling shifts or rotas. Variable shifts and night shifts may be particularly problematic for an employee trying to maintain her milk supply. A breastfeeding employee should not be required to attend training courses or meetings that will involve an excessively long working day or nights spent away from home.

Suggested clauses for a Maternity and Parental Rights Policy

Post-natal care and breastfeeding

Legal minimum	Best practice options
[...employer...] will protect the health and safety of a breastfeeding mother and her baby and of a mother who has given birth in the last six months. [...employer...] will provide adequate rest, meal and refreshment breaks for employees who have recently given birth or are breastfeeding.	If you wish you will normally be allowed [flexible working hours for a period of [weeks/months] after maternity leave] [to return to work gradually over a period of [weeks/months]] in order to adjust to being back at work and/or continue breastfeeding. If on returning to work you are continuing to breastfeed, up to [one] hour a day will be available, in addition to lunch hour, either for you to feed your baby or to express milk. A warm, comfortable, private room can be found in [ ]. Employees who have recently given birth [are entitled to [5] days' paid time off] [may take time off as part of family leave] for postnatal care, e.g. attendance at health clinics.

CHAPTER 7

Parental rights

7.1 PATERNITY LEAVE

> **Paternity leave**
>
> There is no legal right to paternity leave (time off for fathers around the birth) but some employers offer it.
>
> Fathers now have a legal right to unpaid parental leave which can be taken when a baby is born (see 'Parental leave', below).

Paternity leave for fathers around the birth

There is no legal right to paternity leave at present although many employers give a contractual right to paid or unpaid time off around the time the baby is born. Contractual paternity leave can be in addition to any parental leave (see 'Parental leave', below).

An employment tribunal recently found that a man who was sacked after he took a small amount of unauthorised time off to attend the birth of his child had been unfairly dismissed and awarded him compensation.

A father who wants to be present at the birth could book parental leave (after giving his employer notice), or if his partner went into labour at short notice he would be entitled to reasonable time off for urgent care of dependants (see 'Time off for dependants', below).

Suggested clauses for a Maternity and Parental Rights Policy

Paternity leave

Legal minimum	Best practice options
There is no right to paternity leave, but you can take part of your parental leave when your baby is born.	The father or nominated carer of a child is entitled to [10] days' fully paid paternity leave to be taken at the time of the birth. Requests for further unpaid leave will be seriously considered.

7.2   TIME OFF FOR DEPENDANTS

> **Time off for dependants**
>
> **All employees have the right to time off for urgent family reasons in the event of sickness or accident.**

Reasonable time off

All employees, regardless of length of service, have the right to take reasonable unpaid time off which is necessary to deal with the urgent care of a dependant and to make any longer term arrangements (ERA 1996, s57A). Urgent care of a dependant may include:

- providing assistance when a dependant falls ill, gives birth or is injured;

- making arrangements for the provision of care for a dependant who is ill or injured;

- dealing with unexpected disruption or termination of care arrangements of a dependant, e.g. a childminder falls ill; or

- dealing with an incident which occurs unexpectedly in a period in which a child is at school or nursery.

There is no legal definition of what amounts to 'reasonable' time off and, as yet, there is no case law which clarifies the full extent of the new entitlement. What is reasonable will depend on the circumstances in each case but it has to be 'necessary' for the employee to take the time off, for example, an accident or emergency. The leave should be enough to deal with the immediate care of the dependant and make any longer term care arrangements necessary. It would not, for instance, entitle an employee to have two weeks off to look after a sick child unless there was a good reason why the child could not be left, e.g. s/he was very distressed.

Some employers already pay employees for emergency time off at their discretion. Generally speaking, an employer cannot take away a contractual right to paid leave without their employee's agreement. Nonetheless, all employees are now entitled to reasonable unpaid time off for dependants.

Definition of a dependant

A dependant is the husband, wife, child or parent of the employee and may also include someone who lives in the same household as the employee such as an elderly relative. In cases of illness or injury, a dependant may be someone who reasonably relies on the employee for assistance, where the employee is the primary carer or the only person who can help in an emergency.

Notifying the employer

Employees must tell their employer, as soon as practicable, the reason for their absence and how long they expect to be away from work. Where it has not been possible to contact the employer before returning to work, the employee should tell the employer the reason for the absence on return.

Resolving a dispute

If there is a dispute about time off for the care of a dependant or the employer believes an employee is abusing the right to time off, the employer and employee should deal with the situation according to their normal grievance and disciplinary procedures.

Legal action

An employee can bring a claim in an employment tribunal if they have been penalised or dismissed for taking time off for urgent care of a dependant (1999 Regulations, Regs 19 and 20).

Suggested clauses for a Maternity and Parental Rights Policy

Time off for dependants

Legal minimum	Best practice options
You have the right to take reasonable unpaid leave to take action which is necessary: • to provide assistance when a dependant falls ill, gives birth, is injured or assaulted, or to deal with the death of a dependant; • to make arrangements for the care for a dependant who is ill or injured; • to deal with the unexpected disruption or termination of arrangements for the care of a dependant, or to deal with an incident which involves a dependant and which occurs unexpectedly in a period during which an educational establishment which the child attends is responsible for him/her. You must notify [...employer...] as soon as practicable of the reason for your absence and how long you expect to be away from work.	You are entitled to up to [15] days' paid leave per year for family responsibilities. This includes, but is not limited to, caring for sick dependants, school appointments, dealing with childcare problems, and leave for compassionate reasons. You must give as much notice as possible before you take time off for dependants and must provide full details of what you require it for and when you expect to return to work. Further reasonable periods of unpaid leave will be granted if it is necessary to deal with an emergency involving a dependant and to make arrangements for the care of the dependant. You must notify [...employer...] as soon as practicable of the reason for your absence and how long you expect to be away from work.

7.3 PARENTAL LEAVE

> **Parental leave**
>
> **All parents, including adoptive parents, are entitled to 13 weeks' unpaid parental leave, to be taken within five years of the child's birth, adoption or placement for adoption.**

Entitlement to parental leave

Parental leave is for parents with babies born or placed for adoption on or after 15 December 1999 (1999 Regulations, Part III). Both parents are entitled to parental leave for each child. Employees are entitled to parental leave if:

- they have been employed for a year;

- they have or expect to have responsibility for a child (defined as being on the birth certificate or having a parental responsibility order);

- they take leave for the purpose of caring for a child.

New employees can carry over parental leave that has not been taken from one job to the next. Employers can ask new employees and their previous employer how much parental leave has been taken so far. A new employee would have to work for one year in order to qualify for parental leave (unless the employer offers more generous parental leave than the default scheme).

Parental leave schemes

Employers and their employees are encouraged to negotiate the details of a parental leave policy in a collective agreement or workforce agreement (1999 Regulations, Sch. 1). The 1999 Regulations set out the legal minimum and a 'default scheme' (1999 Regulations, Reg. 16 and Sch. 2) which applies if there is no collective or workforce agreement in place.

Duration of parental leave

Parental leave is 13 weeks for each parent for each individual child:

- to be taken by the child's fifth birthday or, in the case of a child placed for adoption, within five years of placement for adoption or the child's 18th birthday, whichever is earlier;

- in the case of a child entitled to disability living allowance (DLA), parental leave can be taken up to the child's 18th birthday.

Terms and conditions during parental leave

The contract of employment continues and the following terms and conditions apply:

- duties of trust and confidence and good faith;

- grievance and disciplinary procedures;

- notice and redundancy pay;

- statutory holiday under the Working Time Regulations 1998.

There is no obligation for an employer to pay an employee who is on parental leave. Contractual rights, such as the right to a company car, do not continue unless agreed.

Returning to work after parental leave

- No notice of return is required.

- An employee has the right to return to the same job at the end of parental leave of four weeks or less (except when parental leave has been taken at the end of additional maternity leave).

- If an employee takes parental leave of four weeks or less immediately after the end of AML and it was not reasonably practicable for her to return to the same job at the end of AML, the employer must offer her suitable alternative work on similar terms and conditions (see 'Return to work after AML', Chapter 6).

- If an employee takes parental leave of more than four weeks and it is not reasonably practicable for them to return to the same job, s/he must be offered suitable alternative work on similar terms and conditions.

Default scheme

Where there is no collective or workforce agreement, the default scheme applies which sets out how and when parental leave can be taken (1999 Regulations, Reg. 16, see Appendix). None of the provisions below need apply if a workforce agreement is reached. Employers can improve on any of these terms with individuals if they wish.

Length of parental leave

- Parental leave must be taken in blocks of a week or more (unless the child is entitled to disability living allowance).

- The maximum annual leave allowance is four weeks in respect of any individual child during a particular year.

Notice to take parental leave

- An employee must give at least 21 days' notice that they wish to take parental leave.

Postponement of leave:

- An employer may postpone the leave for up to six months at the most but only if the business would be unduly disrupted.

- BUT fathers and adoptive parents who want to guarantee that they can be present at the birth/adoption may book time off without postponement.

An employer must notify the employee of postponement within seven days of the employees notice to take parental leave.

Proof: an employer may make a reasonable request for proof that an employee is entitled to parental leave (e.g. birth certificate, maternity certificate showing the EWC, parental responsibility order, proof of adoption, proof of child's entitlement to disability living allowance).

Legal action

Employees can make a complaint to an employment tribunal if they have been unreasonably refused or prevented from taking parental leave, or have been treated unfairly or dismissed for taking parental leave (ERA 1996, s47C; 1999 Regulations, Regs 19 and 20).

Suggested clauses for a Maternity and Parental Rights Policy

Parental leave

	LEGAL MINIMUM – DEFAULT OPTION	GOOD PRACTICE OPTIONS
Entitlement to parental leave	You qualify for parental leave if you: • have worked for your employer for a year or more by the date you are due to start your leave • have or expect to have responsibility for a child • you are taking leave for the purpose of caring for a child that was born or placed for adoption after 15 December 1999.	You qualify for parental leave if you: • have or expect to have responsibility for a child • you are taking leave for the purpose of caring for a child.
When parental leave may be taken	You may take parental leave: • up to the child's fifth birthday, except: • if the child is entitled to disability living allowance, up to the child's 18th birthday. • if the child has been placed for adoption, up to the fifth anniversary of the adoption or their 18th birthday, whichever is the earlier.	You may take parental leave: Up to the child's [eighth] [eleventh] [eighteenth] birthday except: • if the child is entitled to disability living allowance, up to the child's 18th birthday • if the child has been placed for adoption, up to the [fifth] [eighth] [11th] anniversary of the adoption or their 18th birthday, whichever is the earlier.
Duration of parental leave	Parental leave is available to you for a maximum of thirteen weeks.	Parental leave is available for a maximum of [13] [26] weeks. [In the case of adoptive parents (who do not qualify for maternity leave and pay), parental leave is available for [31] [53] weeks.]

Taking parental leave	Parental leave may be taken [up to four weeks a year] [in blocks of a week or more at a time, up to four weeks a year]. You must give 21 days' notice.	Parental leave may be taken in blocks of a day [half a day or more. [Notice must be given as follows: • seven days for blocks of a week or less • 21 days for blocks of more than a week • if it is not possible to give the correct notice, notice must be given as soon as reasonably practicable.] [Parental leave can be booked in the same way as annual leave and the same amount of notice given.]
Postponing parental leave	A request for parental leave can be postponed for up to six months if your absence would cause undue disruption to the business except for leave to be present at the birth or when a child is placed for adoption.	[...employer...] will not postpone your parental leave except in exceptional circumstances. Leave to be present at the birth or when a child is placed for adoption will never be postponed [and neither will leave that an employee plans to take at the end of maternity or paternity leave]. Note: efforts should be made to agree a postponement policy so that guidelines are set down before the event.
Salary/wages during parental leave	Parental leave is unpaid.	During your parental leave you will be paid your [half your] normal salary/wages which will include any allowances or bonuses normally payable during that time.

Terms and conditions during parental leave	You will continue to be an employee during parental leave and both you and your employer will continue to be bound by the rights and duties of employer and employee, but many of the contractual benefits that you normally receive under your contract (e.g. health insurance) will not apply.	You will continue to be an employee during parental leave and all your normal terms and conditions of employment will continue to apply.
Returning to work after parental leave	If you take four weeks or less, you have the right to return to the same job. If you take more than four weeks (under a collective/workforce agreement) or if you take your parental leave immediately after AML and it is not feasible to return to the same job (or would not have been feasible after AML), you have the right to return to a suitable alternative on similar terms and conditions.	You have the right to return to the same job you had before the start of your parental leave.

Maternity and Parental Rights – A Practical Guide

CHAPTER 8

Maternity and parental rights policies

8.1 POLICY DECISIONS

Working parents: facts and figures

- In 1999, there were 5.7 million households with at least one child under 12. In two-thirds of couples with dependant children, both partners worked (Labour Force Survey, Autumn 1999).

- 55% of pregnant women work during pregnancy. This represents about 403,000 babies a year born to working mothers (Callendar *et al.*, '*Maternity Rights and Benefits in Britain in 1996*, DSS Research Report No. 67).

- Overall, two-thirds (67%) of women returned to work. 86% of women went back to work for their previous employer after childbirth. Two-thirds of women returning to their previous employer after childbirth do so on a part-time basis (Callendar *et al.*).

- 20% of employers offer some form of contractual maternity pay. The higher the job status, the more likely a woman is to get contractual maternity pay, which is received by 45% of women in professional jobs compared with just 5% of women in sales jobs (Callendar *et al.*).

- A 1999 MORI survey found that 22% of parents would like more flexible working hours and that 17% of parents find their working hours problematic. It also found that only 17% of parents have employers who offer incentives to encourage mothers back to work after having a baby (MORI 1999).

Good employment practices: the business case

- Women are more likely to return to work if they work for an employer operating family-friendly policies (77%). Women were least likely to return where their employer had no such policies (56%) (Callendar et al.).

- 74% of the UK's top 500 companies agree that there is a recognised business case for introducing family-friendly policies (MORI 1998).

- A publishing company with 500 (mainly women) employees saved £50,000 in re-training costs by offering better maternity provision, family leave and support for childcare. An IT business with 300 employees has found that using family-friendly work practices has reduced the amount of casual sickness absence (*Family-friendly employment – the business case*, DfEE Research Report No. 136, 1999, Bovan, S., Dench, S., Tamkin, P., and Cummins, J.).

- In a survey of the FTSE 100 companies, 65% offered maternity leave and pay above the statutory minimum and 96% offered part-time work. Over a quarter of the companies assessed were rated as having very good family-friendly employment policies and those companies outperformed other companies in terms of significantly higher share performance (Family Friendly Employment Survey, Rathbone Neilson Cobbold, 1998).

Reasons for offering enhanced maternity and parental rights

Some of the main reasons for offering enhanced rights have been found to be:

- retention of experienced staff;
- recruitment of skilled staff;
- equal opportunities;
- reduced turnover, recruitment and training costs;
- reduced absenteeism and sickness absence;
- improved staff morale and productivity;
- higher return after childbirth;
- simplified administration and reduced costs.

Enhanced maternity and parental rights

The enhanced terms that are most commonly offered include the following:

- improved leave;
- improved pay;

- reduction or removal of qualifying service periods where applicable;

- additional pay on condition of a qualifying service period or return to work for a specified period;

- returner's bonus;

- retention of benefits during leave.

Decisions to be made when constructing a maternity and parental policy

Employers may decide to offer a maternity and parental policy that incorporates the legal minimum to which employees are entitled. In areas where the law is unclear, employers will need to make a policy decision on what to include. Areas where the law is unclear are indicated in the text of the policy below. See Section 8.2 for an example of a legal minimum Maternity and Parental Policy.

Employers who wish to upgrade and improve on the minimum legal entitlement will need to weigh up the costs and benefits of offering enhanced rights. See Section 8.3 for an example of a Best Practice Maternity and Parental Policy.

8.2   SUGGESTED MATERNITY AND PARENTAL RIGHTS POLICY: LEGAL MINIMUM

Statement of intent

No employee will be treated less favourably or dismissed because she is pregnant, absent on maternity leave, because she is breastfeeding or for any other reason connected with her pregnancy or maternity.

The rights and obligations set out in this policy apply equally to full-time and part-time workers, regardless of hours worked or length of service.

Health and safety during pregnancy

Once you have notified [...employer...] that you are pregnant (see 'Telling your employer you are pregnant', below), breastfeeding or have given birth recently (see 'Postnatal health and safety and breastfeeding', below [...employer...] will take the following steps to protect your health and safety:

STEP 1 Carry out a 'risk assessment' of any processes, working conditions or agents which could jeopardise your health or safety or that of your baby.

STEP 2 If a significant risk is found, do all that is reasonable to remove it or prevent exposure to it.

STEP 3 Give information on the risk and what action has been taken.

STEP 4 If the risk remains, temporarily alter your working conditions or hours of work, if this is reasonable and if this avoids the risk.

STEP 5 If the risk cannot be avoided, offer you suitable alternative work (on terms and conditions which are not substantially less favourable than your original job).

STEP 6 If there is no suitable alternative work available, you will be suspended on full pay for as long as is necessary to avoid the risk.

Antenatal care

You are entitled not to be unreasonably refused paid time off during working hours for antenatal care. After the first appointment, if requested, you must produce a doctor's certificate confirming that you are pregnant and written proof of the appointment. Please try to arrange absences to minimise disruption to your work. [Policy decision: employers need to define antenatal care, see Chapter 2, e.g. antenatal care includes attendance at relaxation and parentcraft classes made on the recommendation of your GP or midwife.]

Stillbirth

If your baby is stillborn after the 24th week of pregnancy, you still qualify for all the rights described in this policy.

Sickness during pregnancy

You will not be dismissed for having a pregnancy-related illness. If you are sick during pregnancy, [...employer...]'s normal sick pay policy applies and you must notify [...employer...] that you are unwell in the usual way.

Telling [...employer...] you are pregnant

The latest you can tell [...employer...] is 21 days before you go on maternity leave (see 'Notice to start maternity leave and pay', below). However, please tell us as soon as you feel able – until you tell us we cannot take steps to protect your health and safety. The law protects you from being dismissed or discriminated against on the grounds of pregnancy.

Maternity leave

You may take up to 18 weeks' ordinary maternity leave regardless of your length of service or hours worked.

You may not return to work for two weeks after the day the baby is born. If you have been employed continuously for at least one year and 11 weeks by the start of the expected week of childbirth (EWC), you are entitled to take additional maternity leave (AML) which begins at the end of ordinary maternity leave (OML) and ends up to 29 weeks from the start of the week your baby is born.

The start of maternity leave

Your leave cannot start earlier than the 11th week before EWC. After that you are entitled to start your leave and any maternity pay you are entitled to on the date given in your notice unless:

- your baby is born before your leave is due to start (in which case your leave will start on the actual date of birth of your baby even if that is before the 11th week before the EWC); or

- you are absent from work wholly or partly because of pregnancy after the beginning of the sixth week before the EWC (your leave will start on the first day of pregnancy-related absence).

Notice for start of maternity leave and pay

You must give a minimum of 21 days' notice before you start your maternity leave. Your notice should state:

1) that you are pregnant;

2) the date of your EWC (or the date of birth if this has already occurred);

3) the date you intend to start your leave;

4) you must enclose your MATB1;

5) you should confirm your request for maternity pay.

If you cannot give notice, you must make sure you give notice as soon as you reasonably can. [You do not have to give notice in writing but it is advisable] [you must give notice in writing if requested.]

Statutory maternity pay

You are entitled to receive SMP at the rate of 90% of your average pay for six weeks and a flat rate of £62.20 (from April 2001–April 2002) for up to 12 weeks if:

- you have 26 weeks' continuous service at the 15th week before the EWC; and

- you are still in your job in that 15th week; and

- your average earnings are not below the lower earnings limit (£72 from April 2001–April 2002); and

- you stop work because of pregnancy or you had to leave work involuntarily for reasons unconnected to pregnancy.

If you are not entitled to SMP, we will give you a form SMP1 explaining why. If you have been working and earning at least £30 a week, you may qualify for maternity allowance or incapacity benefit from the Benefits Agency instead.

Rights during maternity leave

Throughout your maternity leave

- your contract of employment continues BUT you are not necessarily entitled to all your normal terms and conditions;

- your continuity of employment is preserved so that the time you are away is not counted as a break in your employment;

- you are entitled to be considered for training, career development and promotion opportunities, etc.;

- you are entitled to the proportion of any bonus you earned whilst at work; and

- you are entitled to the full statutory holiday of 20 days' paid leave a year.

During OML

- you are entitled to the benefit of your normal terms and conditions of employment – apart from normal pay. For example, you may keep your company car/car allowance and holidays over and above the statutory minimum will continue to accrue. [Policy decision: employers need to define normal pay. See 'Rights during maternity leave', Chapter 5.]

During AML

- your period of AML will not count towards length of service for contractual purposes, e.g. annual increment;

- you are only entitled to the benefit of some of your normal terms and conditions of employment, but the following apply:

  - notice period for termination of employment;

  - compensation in the event of redundancy;

  - disciplinary and grievance procedures;

  - implied term of trust and confidence;

  - duty of confidentiality;

  - obligation to act in good faith;

  - any terms relating to acceptance of gifts or benefits or participation in any other business.

[Policy decision: employers may wish to continue giving contractual rights during AML as a refusal may be open to challenge under sex discrimination law. See 'Rights during maternity leave', Chapter 5.]

Pensions

Pension contributions at the normal rate will be paid by [...employer...] for the first 18 weeks of OML and any further period during which you are receiving maternity pay.

If you pay your own contributions, they will be calculated by reference to your actual maternity pay while you are receiving it.

If you have any queries, check your options with the pension company/personnel department.

Redundancy during and after maternity leave

You will not be made redundant for any reason connected to the fact that you have taken maternity leave. If your post becomes redundant during your maternity leave, you are entitled to be offered any suitable alternative post that exists in the organisation.

If no alternative exists, [...employer...]'s normal redundancy policy applies. In most cases, you will be entitled to full notice pay.

Returning to work

Returning after OML (18 weeks)

You do not need to give notice that you intend to return to work. You have the right to return to exactly the same job. If you want to return to work *before* the end of your maternity leave, you must give at least 21 days' notice.

Confirmation that you intend to return to work

If you qualify for additional maternity leave, [...employer...] may write to you at any time from 15 weeks after the start of your basic maternity leave asking you to confirm the date your baby was born and that you are returning to work. You must reply in writing within 21 days. There is no penalty if you change your mind later but you must confirm your intention to return.

Returning after AML

You do not need to give notice that you intend to return to work. If you want to return *before* the end of your maternity leave, you must give [...employer...] at least 21 days' written notice of the date you intend to return to work. You have the right to return to the same job or, if that is not reasonably practicable, a suitable job on similar terms and conditions.

Sickness during and after maternity leave

During maternity leave

You are not entitled to sick pay whilst you are on maternity leave although you may be able to claim incapacity benefit from the Benefits Agency.

After maternity leave

Once your maternity leave has ended, if you are unwell and unable to come to work you will be on sick leave in the normal way. You must follow the procedures in [...employer...]'s sickness policy.

If you do not intend to return to work after maternity leave

You must give the notice of resignation normally required by your contract. When you resign, [...employer...] will send you your P45 and will pay you for any holiday that you have not taken including any holiday accrued whilst you have been on maternity leave. You will not have to repay any SMP that you have received.

Return to work on a part-time and/or flexible basis

If your childcare responsibilities make it impossible for you to return to work full time after maternity leave, [...employer...] will seriously consider your request to return to your old job on a part-time and/or flexible basis in the short or long term.

[Policy decision: employers will need a good business reason to refuse the request or the refusal could be indirect sex discrimination, see 'Requests to return to work on different hours', Chapter 6.]

Postnatal care and breastfeeding mothers

[...employer...] will protect the health and safety of a breastfeeding mother and her baby, and of a mother who has given birth in the last six months.

[...employer...] will provide adequate rest, meal and refreshment breaks for women who have recently given birth or are breastfeeding.

Paternity leave

There is no right to paternity leave, but you can take part of your parental leave when your baby is born.

Time off for dependants

You are entitled to reasonable unpaid leave which is necessary in an emergency involving a dependant and to make arrangements for the care of the dependant. You must notify [...employer...] as soon as practicable of the reason for your absence and how long you expect to be away from work.

Parental leave

All parents, including adoptive parents, are entitled not to be unreasonably refused 13 weeks' unpaid parental leave, to be taken within five years of the child's birth. Parental leave may be taken [in blocks of a week, up to four weeks a year] [up to four weeks a year]. [Policy decision: employers may wish to offer more flexible arrangements on length of leave and notice requirements, see 'Parental leave', Chapter 7.]

You must give [...employer...] at least 21 days' notice. [...Employer...] may postpone parental leave for up to six months if it would cause undue disruption to the business except where leave is required to be present at the birth or adoption placement.

Terms and conditions during parental leave

Your contract of employment continues but many of your normal contractual benefits will not apply during parental leave.

Returning to work after parental leave

If you take parental leave of four weeks or less, you are entitled to return to the same job. If you take parental leave of more than four weeks or immediately after additional maternity leave and it is not feasible to return to the same job (or would not have been feasible after AML), you have the right to return to a suitable job on similar terms and conditions.

8.3 SUGGESTED BEST PRACTICE MATERNITY AND PARENTAL RIGHTS POLICY

Statement of intent

No employee will be treated less favourably or dismissed because she is pregnant, absent on maternity leave, because she is breastfeeding or for any other reason connected with her pregnancy or maternity.

The rights and obligations set out in this policy apply equally to full-time and part-time workers, regardless of hours worked or length of service.

The legal status of this policy

The rights and obligations set out here form part of your contract of employment and can only be amended in accordance with it.

Health and safety during pregnancy

Once you have notified [...employer...] that you are pregnant (see 'Telling your employer you are pregnant', below), breastfeeding or have given birth recently (see 'Postnatal care and breastfeeding', below), [...employer...] will take the following steps to protect your health and safety:

STEP 1 Carry out a 'risk assessment' of any processes, working conditions or agents which could jeopardise your health or safety or that of your baby.

STEP 2 If a significant risk is found, do all that is reasonable to remove it or prevent exposure to it.

STEP 3 Give information on the risk and what action has been taken.

STEP 4 If the risk remains, temporarily alter your working conditions or hours of work, if this is reasonable and if this avoids the risk.

STEP 5 If the risk cannot be avoided, offer you suitable alternative work (on terms and conditions which are not substantially less favourable than your original job).

STEP 6 If there is no suitable alternative work available, you will be suspended on full pay for as long as is necessary to avoid the risk.

Antenatal care

You are entitled not to be unreasonably refused paid time off during working hours for antenatal care. After the first appointment, if requested, you must produce a doctor's certificate confirming that you are pregnant and written proof of the appointment. Please try to arrange absences to minimise disruption to your work.

"Antenatal care" includes attendance at relaxation and parentcraft classes on the recommendation of your doctor or midwife.

The partner of a pregnant woman is entitled to paid time-off to attend antenatal appointments.

Stillbirth

If your baby is stillborn after the 24th week of pregnancy you still qualify for all the rights described in this policy.

Sickness during pregnancy

You will not be dismissed for having a pregnancy-related illness. If you are sick during pregnancy [...employer...]'s normal sick pay policy applies and you must notify [...employer...] that you are unwell in the usual way.

Telling [...employer...] you are pregnant

The latest you can tell [...employer...] is 21 days before you go on maternity leave (see 'Notice to start maternity leave and pay', below). However, please tell us as soon as you feel able – until you tell us we cannot take steps to protect your health and safety. The law protects you from being dismissed or discriminated against on the grounds of pregnancy.

Maternity leave

All employees are entitled to [up to 11 weeks off before the EWC and up to [29] [40] [52] weeks after the birth] [up to 52 weeks' leave from the start of maternity leave] regardless of length of service or hours worked. You may not return to work for two weeks after the day your baby is born.

If your baby is born prematurely before the fourth week before the EWC, [you may split your leave and return to work for a period before taking the balance of leave due to you] [you are entitled to an extra week's leave for each full week that your baby is premature].

The start of maternity leave and pay

Your leave cannot start earlier than the 11th week before EWC. After that you are entitled to start your leave and any maternity pay you are entitled to on the date given in your notice. You need not start your leave until the birth unless you choose to start earlier.

Notice for start of maternity leave and pay

You must give a minimum of 21 days' notice before you start your maternity leave. Your notice should state:

1) that you are pregnant;
2) the date of your EWC (or the date of birth if this has already occurred);
3) the date you intend to start your leave;
4) you must enclose your MATB1;
5) you should confirm your request for maternity pay.

If you cannot give notice, you must make sure you give notice as soon as you reasonably can. You do not have to give notice in writing but it is advisable.

A letter for you to use to give notice is on page [***] of this policy.

Maternity pay

You are entitled to [[18] [26] weeks' full pay] [[10] weeks' full pay and [10] weeks' half pay] [regardless of length of service or earnings], inclusive of any SMP you are entitled to, [providing you are still employed until at least the 15th week before your EWC].

[You are entitled to the equivalent of SMP regardless of length of service or earnings, net of any maternity allowance that you can claim.]

Rights during maternity leave

Throughout your maternity leave:

- your contract of employment continues;

- your continuity of employment is preserved so that the time you are away is not counted as a break in your employment;

- you are entitled to be considered for training, career development and promotion opportunities, etc.;

- you are entitled to the full statutory holiday of 20 days' paid leave a year;

- you are entitled to the benefit of your normal terms and conditions of employment – apart from normal pay; for example, you may keep your company car/car allowance and holidays will continue to accrue;

- your period of maternity leave will be counted towards length of service for both your statutory and contractual rights.

Pensions

Pension contributions at the normal rate will be paid by [...employer...] throughout your maternity leave.

If you pay your own contributions, they will be calculated by reference to your actual maternity pay while you are receiving it.

If you have any queries, check your options with the pension company/ personnel department.

Redundancy during and after maternity leave

You will not be made redundant for any reason connected to the fact that you have taken maternity leave. If your post becomes redundant during your maternity leave, you are entitled to be offered any suitable alternative post that exists in the organisation.

If no alternative exists, [...employer...]'s normal redundancy policy applies. You will be entitled to the full amount of notice pay that you would normally receive.

Returning to work

You do not need to give notice that you intend to return to work. If you want to return to work *before* the end of your maternity leave, you must give at least 21 days' notice.

You have the right to return to exactly the same job no matter how much maternity or parental leave you take, provided you give any notice required.

Please keep in touch with us during your maternity leave. We will keep in touch with you, too [by sending you the staff newsletter]. Please let us know when your baby has been born so that we can calculate with you the date your maternity leave ends.

Sickness during and after maternity leave

During maternity leave

You are not entitled to sick pay whilst you are on maternity leave although you may be able to claim incapacity benefit from the Benefits Agency.

After maternity leave

Once your maternity leave has ended, if you are unwell and unable to come to work you will be on sick leave in the normal way. You must follow the procedures in [...employer...]'s sickness policy.

If you do not intend to return to work after maternity leave

You must give the notice of resignation normally required by your contract. When you resign [...employer...] will send you your P45 and will pay you for any holiday that you have not taken including any holiday accrued whilst you have been on maternity leave.

You will not have to repay any contractual maternity pay received [as maternity pay is not repayable even if you do not intend to return to work] [if you return to work for three months or more], but please let us know as soon as possible so that we can plan to recruit a replacement.

Return to work on a part-time and/or flexible basis

If you wish to work different hours after maternity leave, you may do so unless the new arrangement would be detrimental to the needs of the business.

Postnatal care and breastfeeding mothers

[...Employer...] will protect the health and safety of a breastfeeding mother and her baby and of a mother who has given birth in the last six months.

[...Employer...] will provide adequate rest, meal and refreshment breaks for women who have recently given birth or are breastfeeding, together with a room to express milk and facilities for storage.

If you wish, you will normally be allowed [flexible working hours for a period of [weeks/months] after maternity leave] [to return to work gradually over a period of [weeks/months]] in order to adjust to being back at work and/or continue breastfeeding.

If on returning to work you are continuing to breastfeed, up to [one] hour a day will be available, in addition to lunch hour, either for you to feed your baby or to express milk. A warm, comfortable, private room can be found in [ ].

Employees who have recently given birth [are entitled to [5] days' paid time off] [may take time off as part of family leave] for postnatal care, e.g. attendance at health clinics.

Paternity leave

The father or nominated carer of a child is entitled to [10] days' fully paid paternity leave to be taken at the time of the birth. Requests for further unpaid leave will be seriously considered.

Time off for dependants

You are entitled to up to [15] days' paid leave per year for family responsibilities. This includes, but is not limited to, caring for sick dependants, school appointments, dealing with childcare problems and leave for compassionate reasons.

You must give as much notice as possible before you take time off for dependants and must provide full details of what you require it for and when you expect to return to work.

Further reasonable periods of unpaid leave will be granted if it is necessary to deal with an emergency involving a dependant and to make arrangements for the care of the dependant. You must notify [...employer...] as soon as practicable of the reason for your absence and how long you expect to be away from work.

Parental leave

All parents, including adoptive parents, are entitled not to be unreasonably refused 13 weeks' paid parental leave at [full] [half] pay, to be taken within [eight] [11] [18] years of the child's birth or adoption.

Parental leave should be booked in the same way as annual leave. [...Employer...] may postpone parental leave in exceptional circumstances unless leave is required to be present at the birth or adoption placement.

Terms and conditions during parental leave

Your contract of employment continues as well as your normal terms and conditions.

Returning to work after parental leave

You have the right to return to the same job after parental leave.

Adoptive leave

Will be given on comparable terms to maternity and paternity leave.

MATERNITY CHECKLIST

Employee's name

Job title

Date of joining

Manager responsible for implementing the Maternity Policy

MATERNITY LEAVE	
Letter of notification for maternity leave/pay (has she given 21 days' notice of her start date?)	. . . .
MATB1 received	. . . .
Expected week of childbirth (EWC)	. . . .
Entitled to ordinary maternity leave (OML) only?	Yes/No
Entitled to additional maternity leave (AML)? (has she been employed for one year and 11 weeks by the start of the EWC? If so she is entitled to additional maternity leave)	Yes/No
Earliest start date for maternity leave (start of 11th week before EWC)	. . . .
Date she intends to start her leave	. . . .
(Optional) letter sent asking if she is still intending to return (cannot be sent earlier than 15 weeks from the start of maternity leave)	. . . .
Does she intend to return?	Yes/No
Actual date of childbirth (if she is entitled to additional maternity leave, the 29 weeks is counted from the Sunday before this date)	. . . .
Date she is due back to work	. . . .

CONTRACTUAL BENEFITS DURING MATERNITY LEAVE	
Period of entitlement	. . . . . . weeks
Holiday	. . . . days
Car	
Other (specify)	
MATERNITY PAY	
Entitled to statutory maternity pay (SMP)? (has she been employed for 26 weeks by the end of the 15th week before the EWC?)	Yes/No
Current salary	. . . .
Average weekly earnings in the calculation period (does it average at more than the LEL?) (for SMP, calculate her average pay in the eight weeks or two months ending with the end of the 15th week before EWC)	£. . . . .
Higher rate SMP (90% of the average, payable for six weeks)	£. . . . .
Pension contributions to be paid up to	. . . .
Notifications to:	
Payroll	Yes
Pensions	Yes
Line manager	Yes

MATERNITY HEALTH AND SAFETY CHECKLIST

Employee's name

Job title

Manager responsible for implementing the Maternity Policy

Manager responsible for implementing the Health and Safety Policy

Date risk assessment carried out

Expected date of childbirth

Key tasks

POTENTIAL RISKS	(TICK)
Standing	
Lifting	
Carrying	
Travelling	
Movements and postures	
Heat	
Noise	
Chemicals (specify)	
Other (specify)	
Is the employee breastfeeding?	

ACTION REQUIRED	DATE COMPLETED

LETTER TO BE SENT BY AN EMPLOYER TO THEIR EMPLOYEE AS SOON AS POSSIBLE AFTER NOTIFICATION OF PREGNANCY

Dear [employee's name]

I confirm that at our meeting on [insert date] you informed me of your pregnancy. Please find enclosed a copy of the company's Maternity and Parental Rights Policy which outlines your rights and obligations in relation to pregnancy and maternity.

In order to work out exactly what you are entitled to, we need confirmation of the expected week of childbirth in the form of a MATB1 which will be available from your general practitioner or midwife when you are about 26 weeks' pregnant.

As part of its risk assessment procedures, the company keeps under review any health and safety risks to pregnant employees. This will apply to you as soon as you have informed us in writing that you are pregnant. However, you are also responsible for your own health and safety and should take care to avoid any undue risks at work. If you have any immediate concerns, please discuss them with your line manager. You are also entitled to paid time off to attend antenatal appointments.

Please feel free to contact me if you wish to discuss any aspect of this letter or the company's Policy. My direct line is [insert number].

Finally, many congratulations and best wishes for your pregnancy.

Yours sincerely

Copies to: Line Manager
                Payroll

Enclosure: company's Maternity and Parental Rights Policy

LETTER OF NOTICE FOR MATERNITY LEAVE AND PAY WHICH CAN BE INCLUDED IN A MATERNITY POLICY FOR EMPLOYEES TO USE

Dear

Notice of maternity leave and pay

This is to give you 21 days' notice that I am asking for my maternity leave and pay entitlement and to inform you:

1. that I am pregnant

2. that my expected week of childbirth is the
   week beginning   Sunday ....
   [OR, if the baby has already been born]
   my baby was born   on ....

3. that I intend to start my maternity leave on   ....

4. I enclose my maternity certificate (MATB1)

5. I am also asking for maternity pay
   [Delete if not applicable to you.]

SIGNED	....
PRINT NAME	....
JOB TITLE	....
DATE	....

[NOTE: If you are not entitled to SMP, [...employer...] will give you a form SMP1 stating the reasons why. You will need to give the SMP1 to the Benefits Agency to claim maternity allowance.]

USEFUL CONTACTS

ACAS

ACAS have a range of handbooks on employment practices which can be ordered from ACAS Reader Ltd, PO Box 16, Earl Shilton, Leicester, LE9 8ZZ or by telephone: 01455 852 225.

Department of Education and Employment

The DfEE has information and publications for employers. *Creating a Work Life Balance*, a good practice guide for employers, can be obtained from the DfEE orderline: 0845 6022260. The DfEE web site has information for employers: www.dfee.gov.uk.

Department of Trade and Industry

The DTI publishes a range of booklets on employment legislation which can be obtained free of charge from Job Centres and Employment Service offices or from the DTI Orderline: 0870 150 2500.

Regulatory guidance can also be found on the DTI web site at www.dti.gov.uk.

The DTI Parental Leave enquiry line gives general advice on parental leave: 020 7215 6207.

Disability Rights Commission

The DRC can advise employees, employers and service providers on the Disability Discrimination Act 1995 and on how to implement good practice. Address: 2nd Floor, Arndale House, The Arndale Centre, Manchester, M43 AQ. Helpline: 08457 622 633.

Equal Opportunities Commission

The EOC can advise employees, employers and advisers on the Sex Discrimination Act 1975. Address: Arndale House, Arndale Centre, Manchester, M4 3EQ. Telephone: 0161 833 9244.

Equalities Commission – Northern Ireland

Andras House, 60 Great Victoria Street, Belfast, BT2 7BB. Telephone: 02890 500600.

Inland Revenue Employers' Helpline

A helpline for employers on all aspects of National Insurance including SMP, SSP, general PAYE inclusive of P11D, Tax Credits, Student Loan repayments and basic VAT registration: 0845 7 143 143. Employers orderline for SMP manuals and calculation tables: 0845 7 646 646.

Institute of Employment Studies

IES have published research on family-friendly practices. IES orderline: 0845 6022260.

Maternity Alliance

The Maternity Alliance has an extensive range of publications on maternity and parental rights. For a full publications list, send a stamped self-addressed envelope to: 45 Beech Street, London EC2P 2LX. The Maternity Alliance also provides an information line for employers, advisers and health professionals on all aspects of maternity and parental rights. The information line is 0845 6013386. Individual enquiries can also be dealt with by letter, fax (020 7588 8584) and by email (info@maternityalliance.org.uk). Information is also available on the web site: www.maternityalliance.org.uk.

New Ways to Work

Advice on flexible working practices. Address: 2nd Floor, 22 Northumberland Avenue, London, WC2N 5AP. Telephone: 020 7930 3755.

Parents at Work

Advice for employers on employees' childcare needs. Address: 45 Beech Street, London, EC2P 8AD. Telephone: 020 7628 3578.

APPENDIX A

∙ ∙

THE MATERNITY AND PARENTAL LEAVE ETC. REGULATIONS 1999, 1999 STATUTORY INSTRUMENT NO. 3312

STATUTORY INSTRUMENTS

1999 No. 3312

TERMS AND CONDITIONS OF EMPLOYMENT

The Maternity and Parental Leave etc. Regulations 1999

Made - - - - -	*10th December 1999*
Coming into force - -	*15th December 1999*

Whereas a draft of the following Regulations was laid before Parliament in accordance with section 236(3) of the Employment Rights Act 1996(**a**) and approved by a resolution of each House of Parliament:

Now, therefore, the Secretary of State, in exercise of the powers conferred on him by sections 47C(2) and (3), 71(1) to (3) and (6), 72(1) and (2), 73(1), (2), (4) and (7), 74(1), (3) and (4), 75(1), 76(1), (2) and (5), 77(1) and (4), 78(1), (2) and (7), 79(1) and (2) and 99(1)(**b**) of that Act and of all other powers enabling him in that behalf, hereby makes the following Regulations:—

PART 1

GENERAL

Citation and commencement

   1. These Regulations may be cited as the Maternity and Parental Leave etc. Regulations 1999 and shall come into force on 15th December 1999.

Interpretation

   2.—(1) In these Regulations—

"the 1996 Act" means the Employment Rights Act 1996;

"additional maternity leave" means leave under section 73 of the 1996 Act;

"business" includes a trade or profession and includes any activity carried on by a body of persons (whether corporate or unincorporated);

"child" means a person under the age of eighteen;

"childbirth" means the birth of a living child or the birth of a child whether living or dead after 24 weeks of pregnancy;

"collective agreement" means a collective agreement within the meaning of section 178 of the Trade Union and Labour Relations (Consolidation) Act 1992(**c**), the trade union parties to which are independent trade unions within the meaning of section 5 of that Act;

(**a**) 1996 c. 18; section 236(3) was amended by paragraph 42 of Part III of Schedule 4 to the Employment Relations Act 1999 (c. 26).
(**b**) Section 47C of the Employment Rights Act 1996 was inserted by paragraph 8 of Part III of Schedule 4 to the Employment Relations Act 1999; sections 71 to 79 of the 1996 Act were substituted by section 7 and Part I of Schedule 4 to the 1999 Act, and section 99 of the 1996 Act was substituted by paragraph 16 of Part III of Schedule 4 to the 1999 Act. The word "prescribed" in section 47C of the 1996 Act is defined in subsection (2) of that section; the same word in sections 71 to 73 is defined in section 75(2), and in section 99 it is defined in subsection (2) of that section.
(**c**) 1992 c. 52.

1

"contract of employment" means a contract of service or apprenticeship, whether express or implied, and (if it is express) whether oral or in writing;

"disability living allowance" means the disability living allowance provided for in Part III of the Social Security Contributions and Benefits Act 1992(**a**);

"employee" means an individual who has entered into or works under (or, where the employment has ceased, worked under) a contract of employment;

"employer" means the person by whom an employee is (or, where the employment has ceased, was) employed;

"expected week of childbirth" means the week, beginning with midnight between Saturday and Sunday, in which it is expected that childbirth will occur, and "week of childbirth" means the week, beginning with midnight between Saturday and Sunday, in which childbirth occurs;

"job", in relation to an employee returning after additional maternity leave or parental leave, means the nature of the work which she is employed to do in accordance with her contract and the capacity and place in which she is so employed;

"ordinary maternity leave" means leave under section 71 of the 1996 Act;

"parental leave" means leave under regulation 13(1);

"parental responsibility" has the meaning given by section 3 of the Children Act 1989(**b**), and "parental responsibilities" has the meaning given by section 1(3) of the Children (Scotland) Act 1995(**c**);

"workforce agreement" means an agreement between an employer and his employees or their representatives in respect of which the conditions set out in Schedule 1 to these Regulations are satisfied.

(2) A reference in any provision of these Regulations to a period of continuous employment is to a period computed in accordance with Chapter I of Part XIV of the 1996 Act, as if that provision were a provision of that Act.

(3) For the purposes of these Regulations any two employers shall be treated as associated if—

(a) one is a company of which the other (directly or indirectly) has control; or

(b) both are companies of which a third person (directly or indirectly) has control;

and "associated employer" shall be construed accordingly.

(4) In these Regulations, unless the context otherwise requires,—

(a) a reference to a numbered regulation or schedule is to the regulation or schedule in these Regulations bearing that number;

(b) a reference in a regulation or schedule to a numbered paragraph is to the paragraph in that regulation or schedule bearing that number, and

(c) a reference in a paragraph to a lettered sub-paragraph is to the sub-paragraph in that paragraph bearing that letter.

Application

3.—(1) The provisions of Part II of these Regulations have effect only in relation to employees whose expected week of childbirth begins on or after 30th April 2000.

(2) Regulation 19 (protection from detriment) has effect only in relation to an act or failure to act which takes place on or after 15th December 1999.

(3) For the purposes of paragraph (2)—

(a) where an act extends over a period, the reference to the date of the act is a reference to the last day of that period, and

(b) a failure to act is to be treated as done when it was decided on.

(4) For the purposes of paragraph (3), in the absence of evidence establishing the contrary an employer shall be taken to decide on a failure to act—

(a) when he does an act inconsistent with doing the failed act, or

---

(**a**) 1992 c. 4.
(**b**) 1989 c. 41.
(**c**) 1995 c. 36.

2

(b) if he has done no such inconsistent act, when the period expires within which he might reasonably have been expected to do the failed act if it was to be done.

(5) Regulation 20 (unfair dismissal) has effect only in relation to dismissals where the effective date of termination (within the meaning of section 97 of the 1996 Act) falls on or after 15th December 1999.

PART II

MATERNITY LEAVE

Entitlement to ordinary maternity leave

4.—(1) An employee is entitled to ordinary maternity leave provided that she satisfies the following conditions—

    (a) at least 21 days before the date on which she intends her ordinary maternity leave period to start, or, if that is not reasonably practicable, as soon as is reasonably practicable, she notifies her employer of—

        (i) her pregnancy;

        (ii) the expected week of childbirth, and

        (iii) the date on which she intends her ordinary maternity leave period to start,

        and

    (b) if requested to do so by her employer, she produces for his inspection a certificate from—

        (i) a registered medical practitioner, or

        (ii) a registered midwife,

        stating the expected week of childbirth.

(2) The notification provided for in paragraph (1)(a)(iii)—

    (a) shall be given in writing, if the employer so requests, and

    (b) shall not specify a date earlier than the beginning of the eleventh week before the expected week of childbirth.

(3) Where, by virtue of regulation 6(1)(b), an employee's ordinary maternity leave period commences with the first day after the beginning of the sixth week before the expected week of childbirth on which she is absent from work wholly or partly because of pregnancy—

    (a) paragraph (1) does not require her to notify her employer of the date specified in that paragraph, but

    (b) (whether or not she has notified him of that date) she is not entitled to ordinary maternity leave unless she notifies him as soon as is reasonably practicable that she is absent from work wholly or partly because of pregnancy.

(4) Where, by virtue of regulation 6(2), an employee's ordinary maternity leave period commences with the day on which childbirth occurs—

    (a) paragraph (1) does not require her to notify her employer of the date specified in that paragraph, but

    (b) (whether or not she has notified him of that date) she is not entitled to ordinary maternity leave unless she notifies him as soon as is reasonably practicable after the birth that she has given birth.

(5) The notification provided for in paragraphs (3)(b) and (4)(b) shall be given in writing, if the employer so requests.

Entitlement to additional maternity leave

5. An employee who satisfies the following conditions is entitled to additional maternity leave—

    (a) she is entitled to ordinary maternity leave, and

    (b) she has, at the beginning of the eleventh week before the expected week of childbirth, been continuously employed for a period of not less than a year.

3

Commencement of maternity leave periods

6.—(1) Subject to paragraph (2), an employee's ordinary maternity leave period commences with the earlier of—

  (a) the date which, in accordance with regulation 4(1)(a)(iii), she notifies to her employer as the date on which she intends her ordinary maternity leave period to start, and

  (b) the first day after the beginning of the sixth week before the expected week of childbirth on which she is absent from work wholly or partly because of pregnancy.

(2) Where the employee's ordinary maternity leave period has not commenced by virtue of paragraph (1) when childbirth occurs, her ordinary maternity leave period commences with the day on which childbirth occurs.

(3) An employee's additional maternity leave period commences on the day after the last day of her ordinary maternity leave period.

Duration of maternity leave periods

7.—(1) Subject to paragraphs (2) and (5), an employee's ordinary maternity leave period continues for the period of eighteen weeks from its commencement, or until the end of the compulsory maternity leave period provided for in regulation 8 if later.

(2) Subject to paragraph (5), where any requirement imposed by or under any relevant statutory provision prohibits the employee from working for any period after the end of the period determined under paragraph (1) by reason of her having recently given birth, her ordinary maternity leave period continues until the end of that later period.

(3) In paragraph (2), "relevant statutory provision" means a provision of—

  (a) an enactment, or

  (b) an instrument under an enactment,

other than a provision for the time being specified in an order under section 66(2) of the 1996 Act.

(4) Subject to paragraph (5), where an employee is entitled to additional maternity leave her additional maternity leave period continues until the end of the period of 29 weeks beginning with the week of childbirth.

(5) Where the employee is dismissed after the commencement of an ordinary or additional maternity leave period but before the time when (apart from this paragraph) that period would end, the period ends at the time of the dismissal.

Compulsory maternity leave

8. The prohibition in section 72 of the 1996 Act, against permitting an employee who satisfies prescribed conditions to work during a particular period (referred to as a "compulsory maternity leave period"), applies—

  (a) in relation to an employee who is entitled to ordinary maternity leave, and

  (b) in respect of the period of two weeks which commences with the day on which childbirth occurs.

Exclusion of entitlement to remuneration during ordinary maternity leave

9. For the purposes of section 71 of the 1996 Act, which includes provision excluding the entitlement of an employee who exercises her right to ordinary maternity leave to the benefit of terms and conditions of employment about remuneration, only sums payable to an employee by way of wages or salary are to be treated as remuneration.

Redundancy during maternity leave

10.—(1) This regulation applies where, during an employee's ordinary or additional maternity leave period, it is not practicable by reason of redundancy for her employer to continue to employ her under her existing contract of employment.

4

(2) Where there is a suitable available vacancy, the employee is entitled to be offered (before the end of her employment under her existing contract) alternative employment with her employer or his successor, or an associated employer, under a new contract of employment which complies with paragraph (3) (and takes effect immediately on the ending of her employment under the previous contract).

(3) The new contract of employment must be such that—

    (a) the work to be done under it is of a kind which is both suitable in relation to the employee and appropriate for her to do in the circumstances, and

    (b) its provisions as to the capacity and place in which she is to be employed, and as to the other terms and conditions of her employment, are not substantially less favourable to her than if she had continued to be employed under the previous contract.

Requirement to notify intention to return during a maternity leave period

11.—(1) An employee who intends to return to work earlier than the end of her ordinary maternity leave period or, where she is entitled to additional maternity leave, the end of her additional maternity leave period, shall give to her employer not less than 21 days' notice of the date on which she intends to return.

(2) If an employee attempts to return to work earlier than the end of a maternity leave period without complying with paragraph (1), her employer is entitled to postpone her return to a date such as will secure, subject to paragraph (3), that he has 21 days' notice of her return.

(3) An employer is not entitled under paragraph (2) to postpone an employee's return to work to a date after the end of the relevant maternity leave period.

(4) If an employee whose return to work has been postponed under paragraph (2) has been notified that she is not to return to work before the date to which her return was postponed, the employer is under no contractual obligation to pay her remuneration until the date to which her return was postponed if she returns to work before that date.

Requirement to notify intention to return after additional maternity leave

12.—(1) Where, not earlier than 21 days before the end of her ordinary maternity leave period, an employee who is entitled to additional maternity leave is requested in accordance with paragraph (3) by her employer to notify him in writing of—

    (a) the date on which childbirth occurred, and

    (b) whether she intends to return to work at the end of her additional maternity leave period,

the employee shall give the requested notification within 21 days of receiving the request.

(2) The provisions of regulations 19 and 20, in so far as they protect an employee against detriment or dismissal for the reason that she took additional maternity leave, do not apply in relation to an employee who has failed to notify her employer in accordance with paragraph (1).

(3) A request under paragraph (1) shall be—

    (a) made in writing, and

    (b) accompanied by a written statement—

        (i) explaining how the employee may determine, in accordance with regulation 7(4), the date on which her additional maternity leave period will end, and

        (ii) warning of the consequence, under paragraph (2), of failure to respond to the employer's request within 21 days of receiving it.

PART III

PARENTAL LEAVE

Entitlement to parental leave

13.—(1) An employee who—

    (a) has been continuously employed for a period of not less than a year; and

5

(b) has, or expects to have, responsibility for a child,

is entitled, in accordance with these Regulations, to be absent from work on parental leave for the purpose of caring for that child.

(2) An employee has responsibility for a child, for the purposes of paragraph (1), if—

    (a) he has parental responsibility or, in Scotland, parental responsibilities for the child; or

    (b) he has been registered as the child's father under any provision of section 10(1) or 10A(1) of the Births and Deaths Registration Act 1953(**a**) or of section 18(1) or (2) of the Registration of Births, Deaths and Marriages (Scotland) Act 1965(**b**).

(3) An employee is not entitled to parental leave in respect of a child born before 15th December 1999, except for a child who is adopted by the employee, or placed with the employee for adoption by him, on or after that date.

Extent of entitlement

14.—(1) An employee is entitled to thirteen weeks' leave in respect of any individual child.

(2) Where the period for which an employee is normally required, under his contract of employment, to work in the course of a week does not vary, a week's leave for the employee is a period of absence from work which is equal in duration to the period for which he is normally required to work.

(3) Where the period for which an employee is normally required, under his contract of employment, to work in the course of a week varies from week to week or over a longer period, or where he is normally required under his contract to work in some weeks but not in others, a week's leave for the employee is a period of absence from work which is equal in duration to the period calculated by dividing the total of the periods for which he is normally required to work in a year by 52.

(4) Where an employee takes leave in periods shorter than the period which constitutes, for him, a week's leave under whichever of paragraphs (2) and (3) is applicable in his case, he completes a week's leave when the aggregate of the periods of leave he has taken equals the period constituting a week's leave for him under the applicable paragraph.

When parental leave may be taken

15. An employee may not exercise any entitlement to parental leave in respect of a child—

    (a) except in the cases referred to in paragraphs (b) to (d), after the date of the child's fifth birthday;

    (b) in a case where the child is entitled to a disability living allowance, after the date of the child's eighteenth birthday;

    (c) in a case where the child was placed with the employee for adoption by him (other than a case where paragraph (b) applies), after—

        (i) the fifth anniversary of the date on which the placement began, or

        (ii) the date of the child's eighteenth birthday,

    whichever is the earlier.

    (d) in a case where—

        (i) the provisions set out in Schedule 2 apply, and

        (ii) the employee would have taken leave on or before a date or anniversary referred to in paragraphs (a) to (c) but for the fact that the employer postponed it under paragraph 6 of that Schedule,

    after the end of the period to which the leave was postponed.

Default provisions in respect of parental leave

16. The provisions set out in Schedule 2 apply in relation to parental leave in the case of an employee whose contract of employment does not include a provision which—

    (a) confers an entitlement to absence from work for the purpose of caring for a child, and

    (b) incorporates or operates by reference to all or part of a collective agreement or workforce agreement.

(**a**) 1953 c. 20; sections 10 and 10A were substituted by the Family Law Reform Act 1987 (c. 42), sections 24 and 25.
(**b**) 1965 c. 49; section 18(1) was substituted, and section 18(2) amended, by the Law Reform (Parent and Child) (Scotland) Act 1986 (c. 9).

6

PART IV

PROVISIONS APPLICABLE IN RELATION TO MORE THAN ONE KIND OF ABSENCE

Application of terms and conditions during periods of leave

17.   An employee who takes additional maternity leave or parental leave—

    (a) is entitled, during the period of leave, to the benefit of her employer's implied obligation to her of trust and confidence and any terms and conditions of her employment relating to—

        (i) notice of the termination of the employment contract by her employer;

        (ii) compensation in the event of redundancy, or

        (iii) disciplinary or grievance procedures;

    (b) is bound, during that period, by her implied obligation to her employer of good faith and any terms and conditions of her employment relating to—

        (i) notice of the termination of the employment contract by her;

        (ii) the disclosure of confidential information;

        (iii) the acceptance of gifts or other benefits, or

        (iv) the employee's participation in any other business.

Right to return after additional maternity leave or parental leave

18.—(1) An employee who takes parental leave for a period of four weeks or less, other than immediately after taking additional maternity leave, is entitled to return from leave to the job in which she was employed before her absence.

(2) An employee who takes additional maternity leave, or parental leave for a period of more than four weeks, is entitled to return from leave to the job in which she was employed before her absence, or, if it is not reasonably practicable for the employer to permit her to return to that job, to another job which is both suitable for her and appropriate for her to do in the circumstances.

(3) An employee who takes parental leave for a period of four weeks or less immediately after additional maternity leave is entitled to return from leave to the job in which she was employed before her absence unless—

    (a) it would not have been reasonably practicable for her to return to that job if she had returned at the end of her additional maternity leave period, and

    (b) it is not reasonably practicable for the employer to permit her to return to that job at the end of her period of parental leave;

otherwise, she is entitled to return to another job which is both suitable for her and appropriate for her to do in the circumstances.

(4) Paragraphs (2) and (3) do not apply where regulation 10 applies.

(5) An employee's right to return under paragraph (1), (2) or (3) is to return—

    (a) on terms and conditions as to remuneration not less favourable than those which would have been applicable to her had she not been absent from work at any time since—

        (i) in the case of an employee returning from additional maternity leave (or parental leave taken immediately after additional maternity leave), the commencement of the ordinary maternity leave period which preceded her additional maternity leave period, or

        (ii) in the case of an employee returning from parental leave (other than parental leave taken immediately after additional maternity leave), the commencement of the period of parental leave;

    (b) with her seniority, pension rights and similar rights as they would have been if the period or periods of her employment prior to her additional maternity leave period, or (as the case may be) her period of parental leave, were continuous with her employment following her return to work (but subject, in the case of an employee

7

returning from additional maternity leave, to the requirements of paragraph 5 of Schedule 5 to the Social Security Act 1989(**a**) (equal treatment under pension schemes: maternity)), and

(c) otherwise on terms and conditions not less favourable than those which would have been applicable to her had she not been absent from work after the end of her ordinary maternity leave period or (as the case may be) during her period of parental leave.

Protection from detriment

19.—(1) An employee is entitled under section 47C of the 1996 Act not to be subjected to any detriment by any act, or any deliberate failure to act, by her employer done for any of the reasons specified in paragraph (2).

(2) The reasons referred to in paragraph (1) are that the employee—

    (a) is pregnant;

    (b) has given birth to a child;

    (c) is the subject of a relevant requirement, or a relevant recommendation, as defined by section 66(2) of the 1996 Act;

    (d) took, sought to take or availed herself of the benefits of, ordinary maternity leave;

    (e) took or sought to take—

        (i) additional maternity leave;

        (ii) parental leave, or

        (iii) time off under section 57A of the 1996 Act;

    (f) declined to sign a workforce agreement for the purpose of these Regulations, or

    (g) being—

        (i) a representative of members of the workforce for the purposes of Schedule 1, or

        (ii) a candidate in an election in which any person elected will, on being elected, become such a representative,

    performed (or proposed to perform) any functions or activities as such a representative or candidate.

(3) For the purposes of paragraph (2)(d), a woman avails herself of the benefits of ordinary maternity leave if, during her ordinary maternity leave period, she avails herself of the benefit of any of the terms and conditions of her employment preserved by section 71 of the 1996 Act during that period.

(4) Paragraph (1) does not apply in a case where the detriment in question amounts to dismissal within the meaning of Part X of the 1996 Act.

(5) Paragraph (2)(b) only applies where the act or failure to act takes place during the employee's ordinary or additional maternity leave period.

(6) For the purposes of paragraph (5)—

    (a) where an act extends over a period, the reference to the date of the act is a reference to the last day of that period, and

    (b) a failure to act is to be treated as done when it was decided on.

(7) For the purposes of paragraph (6), in the absence of evidence establishing the contrary an employer shall be taken to decide on a failure to act—

    (a) when he does an act inconsistent with doing the failed act, or

    (b) if he has done no such inconsistent act, when the period expires within which he might reasonably have been expected to do the failed act if it were to be done.

Unfair dismissal

20.—(1) An employee who is dismissed is entitled under section 99 of the 1996 Act to be regarded for the purposes of Part X of that Act as unfairly dismissed if—

    (a) the reason or principal reason for the dismissal is of a kind specified in paragraph (3), or

---

(**a**) 1989 c. 24.

8

(b) the reason or principal reason for the dismissal is that the employee is redundant, and regulation 10 has not been complied with.

(2) An employee who is dismissed shall also be regarded for the purposes of Part X of the 1996 Act as unfairly dismissed if—

(a) the reason (or, if more than one, the principal reason) for the dismissal is that the employee was redundant;

(b) it is shown that the circumstances constituting the redundancy applied equally to one or more employees in the same undertaking who held positions similar to that held by the employee and who have not been dismissed by the employer, and

(c) it is shown that the reason (or, if more than one, the principal reason) for which the employee was selected for dismissal was a reason of a kind specified in paragraph (3).

(3) The kinds of reason referred to in paragraphs (1) and (2) are reasons connected with—

(a) the pregnancy of the employee;

(b) the fact that the employee has given birth to a child;

(c) the application of a relevant requirement, or a relevant recommendation, as defined by section 66(2) of the 1996 Act;

(d) the fact that she took, sought to take or availed herself of the benefits of, ordinary maternity leave;

(e) the fact that she took or sought to take—

(i) additional maternity leave;

(ii) parental leave, or

(iii) time off under section 57A of the 1996 Act;

(f) the fact that she declined to sign a workforce agreement for the purposes of these Regulations, or

(g) the fact that the employee, being—

(i) a representative of members of the workforce for the purposes of Schedule 1, or

(ii) a candidate in an election in which any person elected will, on being elected, become such a representative,

performed (or proposed to perform) any functions or activities as such a representative or candidate.

(4) Paragraphs (1)(b) and (3)(b) only apply where the dismissal ends the employee's ordinary or additional maternity leave period.

(5) Paragraph (3) of regulation 19 applies for the purposes of paragraph (3)(d) as it applies for the purpose of paragraph (2)(d) of that regulation.

(6) Paragraph (1) does not apply in relation to an employee if—

(a) immediately before the end of her additional maternity leave period (or, if it ends by reason of dismissal, immediately before the dismissal) the number of employees employed by her employer, added to the number employed by any associated employer of his, did not exceed five, and

(b) it is not reasonably practicable for the employer (who may be the same employer or a successor of his) to permit her to return to a job which is both suitable for her and appropriate for her to do in the circumstances or for an associated employer to offer her a job of that kind.

(7) Paragraph (1) does not apply in relation to an employee if—

(a) it is not reasonably practicable for a reason other than redundancy for the employer (who may be the same employer or a successor of his) to permit her to return to a job which is both suitable for her and appropriate for her to do in the circumstances;

(b) an associated employer offers her a job of that kind, and

(c) she accepts or unreasonably refuses that offer.

(8) Where on a complaint of unfair dismissal any question arises as to whether the operation of paragraph (1) is excluded by the provisions of paragraph (6) or (7), it is for the employer to show that the provisions in question were satisfied in relation to the complainant.

9

Contractual rights to maternity or parental leave

21.—(1) This regulation applies where an employee is entitled to—

    (a) ordinary maternity leave;

    (b) additional maternity leave, or

    (c) parental leave,

(referred to in paragraph (2) as a "statutory right") and also to a right which corresponds to that right and which arises under the employee's contract of employment or otherwise.

  (2) In a case where this regulation applies—

    (a) the employee may not exercise the statutory right and the corresponding right separately but may, in taking the leave for which the two rights provide, take advantage of whichever right is, in any particular respect, the more favourable, and

    (b) the provisions of the 1996 Act and of these Regulations relating to the statutory right apply, subject to any modifications necessary to give effect to any more favourable contractual terms, to the exercise of the composite right described in sub-paragraph (a) as they apply to the exercise of the statutory right.

Calculation of a week's pay

  22. Where—

    (a) under Chapter II of part XIV of the 1996 Act, the amount of a week's pay of an employee falls to be calculated by reference to the average rate of remuneration, or the average amount of remuneration, payable to the employee in respect of a period of twelve weeks ending on a particular date (referred to as "the calculation date");

    (b) during a week in that period, the employee was absent from work on ordinary or additional maternity leave or parental leave, and

    (c) remuneration is payable to the employee in respect of that week under her contract of employment, but the amount payable is less than the amount that would be payable if she were working,

that week shall be disregarded for the purpose of the calculation and account shall be taken of remuneration in earlier weeks so as to bring up to twelve the number of weeks of which account is taken.

Stephen Byers
Secretary of State
for Trade and Industry

10th December 1999

Regulation 2(1)

WORKFORCE AGREEMENTS

1.   An agreement is a workforce agreement for the purposes of these Regulations if the following conditions are satisfied—

   (a) the agreement is in writing;

   (b) it has effect for a specified period not exceeding five years;

   (c) it applies either—

      (i) to all of the relevant members of the workforce, or

      (ii) to all of the relevant members of the workforce who belong to a particular group;

   (d) the agreement is signed—

      (i) in the case of an agreement of the kind referred to in sub-paragraph (c)(i), by the representatives of the workforce, and in the case of an agreement of the kind referred to in sub-paragraph (c)(ii), by the representatives of the group to which the agreement applies (excluding, in either case, any representative not a relevant member of the workforce on the date on which the agreement was first made available for signature), or

      (ii) if the employer employed 20 or fewer employees on the date referred to in sub-paragraph (d)(i), either by the appropriate representatives in accordance with that sub-paragraph or by the majority of the employees employed by him;

     and

   (e) before the agreement was made available for signature, the employer provided all the employees to whom it was intended to apply on the date on which it came into effect with copies of the text of the agreement and such guidance as those employees might reasonably require in order to understand it in full.

2.   For the purposes of this Schedule—

"a particular group" is a group of the relevant members of a workforce who undertake a particular function, work at a particular workplace or belong to a particular department or unit within their employer's business;

"relevant members of the workforce" are all of the employees employed by a particular employer, excluding any employee whose terms and conditions of employment are provided for, wholly or in part, in a collective agreement;

"representatives of the workforce" are employees duly elected to represent the relevant members of the workforce, "representatives of the group" are employees duly elected to represent the members of a particular group, and representatives are "duly elected" if the election at which they were elected satisfied the requirements of paragraph 3 of this Schedule.

3.   The requirements concerning elections referred to in paragraph 2 are that—

   (a) the number of representatives to be elected is determined by the employer;

   (b) the candidates for election as representatives of the workforce are relevant members of the workforce, and the candidates for election as representatives of a group are members of the group;

   (c) no employee who is eligible to be a candidate is unreasonably excluded from standing for election;

   (d) all the relevant members of the workforce are entitled to vote for representatives of the workforce, and all the members of a particular group are entitled to vote for representatives of the group;

   (e) the employees entitled to vote may vote for as many candidates as there are representatives to be elected, and

   (f) the election is conducted so as to secure that—

      (i) so far as is reasonably practicable, those voting do so in secret, and

      (ii) the votes given at the election are fairly and accurately counted.

SCHEDULE 2   Regulation 16

DEFAULT PROVISIONS IN RESPECT OF PARENTAL LEAVE

Conditions of entitlement

1.   An employee may not exercise any entitlement to parental leave unless—

   (a) he has complied with any request made by his employer to produce for the employer's inspection evidence of his entitlement, of the kind described in paragraph 2;

   (b) he has given his employer notice, in accordance with whichever of paragraphs 3 to 5 is applicable, of the period of leave he proposes to take, and

11

(c) in a case where paragraph 6 applies, his employer has not postponed the period of leave in accordance with that paragraph.

2.   The evidence to be produced for the purpose of paragraph 1(a) is such evidence as may reasonably be required of—

(a) the employee's responsibility or expected responsibility for the child in respect of whom the employee proposes to take parental leave;

(b) the child's date of birth or, in the case of a child who was placed with the employee for adoption, the date on which the placement began, and

(c) in a case where the employee's right to exercise an entitlement to parental leave under regulation 15, or to take a particular period of leave under paragraph 7, depends upon whether the child is entitled to a disability living allowance, the child's entitlement to that allowance.

Notice to be given to employer

3.   Except in a case where paragraph 4 or 5 applies, the notice required for the purpose of paragraph 1(b) is notice which—

(a) specifies the dates on which the period of leave is to begin and end, and

(b) is given to the employer at least 21 days before the date on which that period is to begin.

4.   Where the employee is the father of the child in respect of whom the leave is to be taken, and the period of leave is to begin on the date on which the child is born, the notice required for the purpose of paragraph 1(b) is notice which—

(a) specifies the expected week of childbirth and the duration of the period of leave, and

(b) is given to the employer at least 21 days before the beginning of the expected week of childbirth.

5.   Where the child in respect of whom the leave is to be taken is to be placed with the employee for adoption by him and the leave is to begin on the date of the placement, the notice required for the purpose of paragraph 1(b) is notice which—

(a) specifies the week in which the placement is expected to occur and the duration of the period of leave, and

(b) is given to the employer at least 21 days before the beginning of that week, or, if that is not reasonably practicable, as soon as is reasonably practicable.

Postponement of leave

6.   An employer may postpone a period of parental leave where—

(a) neither paragraph 4 nor paragraph 5 applies, and the employee has accordingly given the employer notice in accordance with paragraph 3;

(b) the employer considers that the operation of his business would be unduly disrupted if the employee took leave during the period identified in his notice;

(c) the employer agrees to permit the employee to take a period of leave—

(i) of the same duration as the period identified in the employee's notice, and

(ii) beginning on a date determined by the employer after consulting the employee, which is no later than six months after the commencement of that period;

(d) the employer gives the employee notice in writing of the postponement which—

(i) states the reason for it, and

(ii) specifies the dates on which the period of leave the employer agrees to permit the employee to take will begin and end,

and

(e) that notice is given to the employee not more than seven days after the employee's notice was given to the employer.

Minimum periods of leave

7.   An employee may not take parental leave in a period other than the period which constitutes a week's leave for him under regulation 14 or a multiple of that period, except in a case where the child in respect of whom leave is taken is entitled to a disability living allowance.

Maximum annual leave allowance

8.   An employee may not take more than four weeks' leave in respect of any individual child during a particular year.

9.   For the purposes of paragraph 8, a year is the period of twelve months beginning—

(a) except where sub-paragraph (b) applies, on the date on which the employee first became entitled to take parental leave in respect of the child in question, or

12

(b) in a case where the employee's entitlement has been interrupted at the end of a period of continuous employment, on the date on which the employee most recently became entitled to take parental leave in respect of that child,

and each successive period of twelve months beginning on the anniversary of that date.

13

These Regulations, together with provisions inserted into the Employment Rights Act 1996 ("the 1996 Act") by the Employment Relations Act 1999, confer new rights to maternity and parental leave. The provisions relating to parental leave implement Council Directive 96/34/EC on the framework agreement on parental leave (OJ No.L145, 19.6.96, p.4).

The provisions relating to ordinary maternity leave are derived from the maternity leave provisions in sections 72-78 of the 1996 Act as originally enacted, although the period of leave provided for is 18 weeks (reg.7(1)) rather than 14 weeks as under the Act. The provisions relating to additional maternity leave replace sections 79–85 of the 1996 Act as originally enacted; the new provisions differ principally in that the new right is a right to leave for a period of 29 weeks from the beginning of the week of childbirth (reg.7(4)) rather than a right to return within such a period, and that the new right is available to women who have been continuously employed for a year (reg.5) rather than for two years. The provision made for compulsory maternity leave (in new section 72 of the 1996 Act and reg.8) implements article 8.2 of the Pregnant Workers Directive (92/85/EEC; OJ No. L348,28.11.92, p.1), replacing the Maternity (Compulsory Leave) Regulations 1994 (S.I. 1994/2479) which originally implemented that provision.

The right to parental leave is available to employees who have been continuously employed for a year and have, or expect to have, parental responsibility (in Scotland, parental responsibilities) for a child (reg.13). The period of leave is 13 weeks (reg.14), and leave must generally be taken before the child's fifth birthday (reg.15, which sets out exceptions including provision for leave to be taken before the eighteenth birthday of a child entitled to a disability living allowance). Schedule 2 to the Regulations sets out provisions requiring that the employer must be notified of any proposal to take parental leave and may postpone it for up to six months; it also provides that (except in the case of a child entitled to a disability living allowance) parental leave may not be taken in periods other than a week or a multiple of a week. These provisions apply only to employees who are not subject to a collective or workforce agreement relating to parental leave.

In relation to both additional maternity leave and parental leave, provision is made for certain contractual rights and obligations to continue during the period of absence (reg.17), and for the employee to return to the same or an appropriate alternative job after that period (reg.18). The Regulations also make provision under sections 47C and 99 of the 1996 Act (both inserted by the Employment Relations Act 1999), identifying the cases where the protection against detriment or dismissal for which those sections provide is applicable (regs.19 and 20). The cases are not only cases connected with maternity or parental leave but also cases connected with the right to time off for dependants under new section 57A of the 1996 Act.

A Regulatory Impact Assessment of the costs and benefits that these Regulations would have is available to the public from Employment Relations 5A, Department of Trade and Industry, 1 Victoria Street, London SW1H 0ET.

14

INDEX

redundancy during and after
  maternity leave 49
return to work 54
return to work on a part-time
  and/or flexible basis 62
rights during maternity leave 44–5
sickness during and after maternity
  leave 56
sickness during pregnancy 22
statutory maternity pay 37–8
stillbirth 21
time off for dependants 69
maternity leave
  additional 28–30
  checklist 91–2
  compulsory 27
  health and safety legislation 17
  maternity and parental rights
    policy 26–7, 80–1, 81–2, 86–7
  not returning to work 56–7
  ordinary 23–7
  pension contributions 45–6
  redundancy during 47–9
  requests to return on different
    hours 57–62
  return to work 51–4
  rights during 41–5
  sex discrimination 6–7, 12
  sickness during and after 55–6
  six week rule 21–2
  unfair dismissal 9–11, 12
maternity pay
  checklist 92
  contractual 38–9
  sex discrimination 7
  statutory 31–8
  maternity rights 1–3, 4
*Maternity rights: a guide for
  employers and employees* 19
Mawkin v. *The Cats Whisker* 60
Meade-Hill v. *British Council* 8
means tested benefits ix
miscarriage 21

New Ways to Work 58, 97
night work 15, 64
notice pay 12, 41, 48
notice of termination 10, 41

O'Neill v. *Governors of St Thomas
  More RCVA Upper School and
  Bedfordshire CC* 6
ordinary maternity leave (OML) vii,
  viii, 23

entitlement 23
length of service 43
maternity and parental rights
  policies 25–6
notice requirements 24–5, 35
pregnancy-related illness 24
premature births 24
preparations 24
remuneration 42–3
return to work ix, 51
start 23–4
terms and condition during 42
ordinary unfair dismissal *see* unfair
  dismissal

parental leave ix, 70
  default scheme 71–2
  duration 70
  entitlement 70
  legal action 72
  maternity and parental rights
    policy 73–5, 84–5, 89–90
  returning to work 71
  schemes 70
  terms and conditions during 70–1
  unfair dismissal and detrimental
    treatment 12
parental rights
  parental leave 70–5
  paternity leave 67
  time off for dependants 68–9
Parents at Work 97
Part-time Workers (Prevention of Less
  Favourable Treatment)
  Regulations 2000 3, 8, 60–1
part-time working 58
  Best Practice guidance 61–2
  indirect sex discrimination 8
  Part-time Workers Regulations 60–1
Patefield v. *Belfast City Council* 5
paternity leave 67
  maternity and parental rights
    policy 67, 84, 89
Pedersen 6
pension contributions
  maternity leave 45–6
  maternity and parental rights
    policy 46, 82, 87
postnatal care, maternity and
parental rights policy 65, 84, 88–9
pregnancy
  antenatal care 19–20
  health and safety 13–18
  miscarriage and stillbirth 20–1

terms and conditions *see* contracts of employment

Thibault 7

time off for antenatal care viii, 19

time off for dependants ix, 68

   definition of dependant 68

   legal action 69

   maternity and parental rights policy 69, 84, 89

   notifying employer 68–9

reasonable time off 68

resolving disputes 69

unfair dismissal and detrimental treatment 12

Treaty of Rome, Article 141 3

unfair dismissal 1, 9, 10, 11, 12

   antenatal care 19

   automatic 9–10, 12

during maternity leave 44

pregnancy-related illness 21

redundancy 47–8, 49

sickness during and after maternity leave 55

unfair treatment 9, 11, 12, 20

Webb 6

working hours

   indirect sex discrimination 7

   requests to return on different hours 57–62

Working Time Regulations 1998, 1, 3, 41, 48–9

Workplace (Health, Safety and Welfare) Regulations 1992 16, 64